Captain James Cook

CAPTAIN COOK

Life and Voyages of the Great Navigator

BY
WALTER BESANT

LONDON
1890

Printed in Australia

First Printing, 2012

ISBN 978-0-9873052-0-6

www.fitzroygardens.com

CONTENTS

CHAPTER I

BIRTH AND EDUCATION

JAMES COOK was born in the little village of Marton, in that part of Yorkshire known as Cleveland. He came into the world on the 27th day of October, in the year 1728. His father, an agricultural labourer, removed by a single step from the lowest level, is said by one writer to have been a native of Northumberland, and by others to have come from the village of Ednam in Roxburghshire, the birthplace of Thomson the poet.

The village of Marton presents few points of interest. The cottage in which Cook was born was taken down a hundred years ago, and part of a great house, which in its turn is now gone, was built over its site. The place is at present occupied by a plantation. The only relic of Cook's childhood is a pump, called Captain Cook's pump, constructed, it is said, by his father. Probably it was the pump in use by the tenants of the cottage. The village consists of a long street of red brick houses, few of them old. The church was rebuilt in 1848, and most of the tombs in the churchyard are new. James seems to have been the second of a large family of seven or eight, or even more. At a very early age he was set to work on the farm of one William Walker, a wealthy yeoman of Marton. Mary Walker, his wife, seems to have taken the trouble to teach the child his letters. This is the origin of the dame's school and the village dame of which so much is made in Hartley Coleridge's Memoir. Mary Walker lived to the age of eighty-nine, dying in the year 1789, ten years after her pupil. It is hoped that this good lady knew that the lad to whom she had shown a little kindness was none other than the great sailor who filled the world with his name.

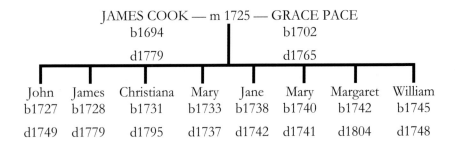

JAMES COOK — m 1725 — GRACE PACE
b1694   b1702

d1779   d1765

John	James	Christiana	Mary	Jane	Mary	Margaret	William
b1727	b1728	b1731	b1733	b1738	b1740	b1742	b1745
d1749	d1779	d1795	d1737	d1742	d1741	d1804	d1748

At the age of eight, in the year 1736, the boy was removed to the village of Great Ayton, between four and five miles south of Marton. Here his father became hind to Mr. Skottowe, then lord of the manor. Great Ayton, which boasts an illustrious roll of proprietors, had passed by marriage from the Coulsons to the Skottowes. It was sold early in the century to a family named Richardson. The word "hind" is generally interpreted to mean bailiff. The practice in the Cleveland district was then, and is still, for the landlord to place a man in charge of a small farm, giving him the farmhouse for his residence, and paying him fixed wages, receiving in return the whole produce of the farm. This tenant or paid labourer is called the landlord's hind. Doubtless this was the position held by James Cook the elder.

At Great Ayton four more children at least were born to the family, and four died and are buried in the churchyard. Here also, in the year 1768, Captain Cook's mother died, aged sixty-three years, happy, we may hope, in the knowledge that one of her sons was in command of a king's ship.

The village of Great Ayton is a much more considerable place than Marton, and far more interesting. It lies close to the north or north-west edge of that splendid stretch of hill and moorland called the Cleveland Hills or the Moors, well known to all who love Whitby and her daughters, the seaside hamlets, each in its glen, built on the slopes of the steep hills beside the sea. The Cleveland Hills begin close to the village of Ayton. North of it runs the long ridge of Langbargh, and east of it rises the picturesque hill called Roseberry Topping, a thousand feet high, crowned with its conical peak of sandstone. Through the village runs a beck, which is crossed by a wide stone bridge. On the south side of the stream, evidently the poorer part of the village, stands the house where Cook's father dwelt. It is said to have been built by him, when he gave up his post as hind and became a stonemason. It is a stone cottage of three or four rooms, with a red-tiled roof, and through the open door one catches a glimpse of a garden behind. Over the door is a stone with the initials J. C. G. and the date 1755. If, as is most probable, these initials mean James Cook and Grace his wife, the house was not built till the son was already twenty-seven years of age and long since flown from the paternal nest. The father was also sixty, and, if he lived here, must have given up his farm.

Cook's biographers grandly tell us that the boy was placed in a day-school at Ayton, and educated at Mr. Skottowe's expense. This seems very magnificent and truly generous on the part of Mr. Skottowe. I believe that this gentleman afterwards proved Cook's friend at the most important juncture in his life, when a single step decided his future. But upon the generosity of the education one need not insist. I have seen the school. It was held on the ground floor of a cottage, built originally, as the inscription above the lintel informs us, in 1704 by one Michael Postgate; it was pulled down in the year 1784, and then rebuilt. The later structure was of exactly the same size as the former. No doubt, as village schools then were, the educational advantages of Great Ayton were considerable, and a boy attending the school from the age of eight to that of twelve may have acquired a good foundation for anything which he might subsequently be able to build upon it. The school has since been refounded and endowed and new buildings have been erected for it, so that it has become a very creditable school indeed.

The village now contains a few old houses and a good number which betoken a certain amount of comfort and wealth. There is a large square with a very good inn. On the other side of the brook is an irregular Place, surrounded by old and somewhat squalid cottages. The old church has been deserted and suffered to fall into decay, and a new church has been built and a new churchyard close to the old. The effect is not pleasing, though the mouldering church, in the midst of its graves, all forgotten and neglected together, is not without its touch of pathos. A monument stands in the churchyard erected by Captain Cook to the memory of his mother. His father, who lived to be eighty-five, died at Redcar on April 1st, 1779, where he lived with his daughter Margaret, who was married to a fisherman there. He is described in the register of deaths as a day-labourer.

The son of a hind of Scotch descent, afterwards a stonemason, and of a Yorkshire woman of like position and parentage, James Cook had little backing from his family and his connections. Yet if we were to have chosen an ancestry which in those days would have given a boy the best chance of success, it would have been difficult to choose a better stock on both sides, on the one hand the Scotch patience, intelligence, and industry, and on the other hand the Yorkshire independence and self-reliance. Add to this a quality, especially essential to success in that century of endurance, hard fare, and continual fighting, the power of contenting himself with the simplest life under the hardest conditions. What the common sailor endured with grumbling Captain Cook endured with cheerfulness. This also he owed as much to his parentage as to the habits of early life.

When the boy reached his thirteenth year, and it was time to look about for him, it was resolved to apprentice him to one Sanderson, a shopkeeper of Staithes or The Staithes. The existence of tombstones in Great Ayton churchyard bearing the name of Sanderson seems to explain why the boy was sent to Mr. Sanderson of Staithes. Perhaps he was in some way connected with the family. Perhaps the Sanderson of Staithes let the Sanderson of Great Ayton know that he was in want of a boy. Certainly the two places were then as far apart and as distinct from each other as York is now from London. In one the population was wholly rural and agricultural, in the other it was wholly seafaring. Between the two villages there lay an expanse more than fifteen miles across. If one wanted a village by the sea, surely Redcar was nearer than Staithes, and Whitby, if one wanted a great commercial centre, was as near. But the boy was sent to Staithes. He would reach it by whatever path led across the moor, probably through Lofthouse, sacred to the memory of a Loathly Worm. No doubt such an apprenticeship would seem to the simple village folk a chance of a rise in the world for their boy. It was indeed a chance, and the lad seized upon it. Yet not quite as they expected.

Along this part of the Yorkshire coast, from Redcar round to Flamborough Head and Bridlington, high cliffs present their faces to the sea, broken at intervals by narrow glens formed by little becks or brooks making their way to the sea. In many of these glens lies nestled a village or a town. Whitby is such a town, built in a narrow valley upon the banks of a stream. Robin Hood's Bay has such a town. Runswick Bay has another. Scarborough is an overgrown example of this kind of fishing village. The Staithes is another example. It is like the rest, built in a narrow valley upon the banks of a little stream. The valley is so narrow and so deep that the place is quite invisible, whether one approaches it by the road or by the cliff. One suddenly turns towards the sea by a steep and winding way and presently discerns the red roofs of the town below. Descending, the road becomes a street, narrow and of evil smell; descending still lower, the street becomes the centre and market of the town, with shops and public-houses; a little farther, and the beach appears, high cliff on either hand; the one on the north running up to a point and breaking down sheer, this is called Coburn Nab, and the other on the south, called Piercey Nab, a more rounded bluff; both are of nearly the same height, namely, just over four hundred feet. A bay is thus formed, partly sheltered from the east, but exposed to the north. "The Staithe" is a wooden pier or sea-wall, not that which was known to James Cook when he became an apprentice here, but one of much more recent construction. Piles of timber have been driven into the ground as far out to sea as possible, in order to make a kind of groyne and to break the force of the waves, which come rolling in from the north with great strength. In the bay there are dozens of boats lying moored side by side; on the shore there are dozens of boats hauled up; the boats in the bay are filled with nets and gear of all kinds; mostly they are painted white with streaks of green, blue, or red; among them are lying, I know not if they came so far a hundred and fifty years ago, the boats of Penzance with their stern sails; you may know them by their rig. In the big smacks half a dozen men go out, but two or three will venture out even in one of the little cobles which are upset so easily unless dexterously managed.

The place appears to be prosperous, though men grumble: on the Staithe the fisher-folk stand about all day long, hands in pocket, pipe in mouth. No Neapolitan could seem lazier; but they are not lazy: they are resting. An hour after midnight they will be on board their craft outward bound for the German Ocean, in all weathers short of a gale, and in all seasons, even when the northeast wind benumbs them with its icy breath. They are not lazy, but ashore they love to sit and stand together all day long, exchanging few words, where the waves wash the beach, and where they scent the fragrance of the fish lying on the shingle above the reach of high tide, and where they can keep an eye upon the open and watch the ships that sail and steam past them on the horizon. There is every indication of a trade by which many do live in comfort; in the town the shops are conducted, though doubtless on a more liberal scale, precisely after the same methods as those prevalent a hundred years ago. That is to say, on one side of the door is the grocery department, and on the other the drapery; so that those who make James Cook apprentice to a draper do not lie, nor do those who make him apprentice to a grocer, since his master, Mr. Sanderson, followed both these trades.

The fisher-folk of the Staithes at the present day are reported to be a moral and virtuous people, largely composed of temperance men; they are further said to be a religious folk belonging to one or other of the many nonconformist Churches represented in the place. The Church of England, which a year or two ago had nothing in the place but an upper chamber rivalling the conventicles in ugliness, is reported, perhaps wrongly, to have a feeble following. The parish church is at Hinderwell on the cliff, a mile and more away; and it is in its churchyard that you will find the tombs of all the master mariners of the Staithes.

In the time when James Cook was apprentice here I suppose that there were none of the dissenting chapels, nonconformity was still a thing of the great towns, and that such of the fisher-folk as had any religion at all walked up the hill on Sundays to Hinderwell. We may easily believe them to have been, like all other fisher and sailor folk of the time, a people given to much drink, but never careless or reckless, that kind of sailor is not common on the coast of Yorkshire. Save in this matter of drink, in which the people are now greatly reformed, the place was much the same then as now. The bright-eyed, clear-skinned girls ran, then as now, lightly along the steep and narrow lanes and courts of the town, carrying baskets of fish on their heads; the wives sat in their porches in their sunbonnets talking and knitting; the men lounged on the Staithe talking all day, if it was fine and not too cold. When it rained or snowed, or when the east wind was too bitter even for their hardy frames, they sat together in the bar of the *Cod and Lobster*, the *Shoulder of Mutton*, and the *Black Lion*, drinking over a pipe of tobacco. On the south side of the main street the narrow courts rose steep and confined, each with its flight of steps; beyond the bay, under Coburn Nab, they were building ships, always one ship at least on the stocks; perhaps a whaler, perhaps a collier, perhaps no more than a fishing smack or a coble; but all day long the cheerful hammer rang, and the shipwrights went in and out among the fisher-folk

He who visits this quaint old Yorkshire town, when he stands upon the far side of the *Cod and Lobster*, upon the wooden pier, may in imagination rebuild a row of houses along the shore exactly similar to those which still stand upon the shore behind him. Such a row actually stood there in the year 1740, and among them was Mr. Sanderson's double shop, the grocery on one side, and the drapery on the other. Under the counter, let us hope that of the latter department, where there would be fewer cockchafers, beetles, and earwigs, slept the apprentice, James Cook. All apprentices slept under the counter in those days. In the morning he swept out the shop, put things in their places, they had not then arrived at dressing the windows; this done, he had his breakfast, a hunch of bread, a lump of fat bacon, and a mug of small ale; this despatched, all day long he fetched, carried, waited, served, and listened to the instructions of Mr. Sanderson. He also listened, whenever he could get outside the shop, to the talk of the seafaring men on the Staithe. He heard many things strange and wonderful; he heard how the men went forth at night in all weathers to catch the herring and the cod; he heard how some of them had served on colliers and coasters, and so knew all the ports and the humours of each from Whitby to Wapping; how some, again, had gone forth to the Arctic seas in whalers and had met with perils many and various among the ice, the bears, and the great whales; nay, there were some who had been pressed into His Majesty's service, fought His Majesty's battles, and returned home again none the worse for their years afloat, even though their backs bore marks of the captain's discipline.

Now to some boys, when they hear such stories, there falls upon their senses a longing so mighty that it overpowers them. Like the rats when the piper of Hamelin first began, like the children when his flute played a second time, they hear strange voices; they see imaginary splendours, the washing of the waves upon the shore falls upon their ears like the sweetest music; their hearts swell only to see a black collier beating up slowly against the wind; and presently a voice not to be resisted calls upon them to arise and betake themselves to some place where they, too, can be received upon shipboard and become sailors for good or for evil. Alas! this was generally, in James Cook's time, for evil; the sailor had then things to encounter the like of which we have now wellnigh forgotten; there was scurvy at sea, there were ships too clumsy to answer helm, there were worm-eaten bottoms, there was foul water to drink and not enough of it, salt junk to eat and not enough of that there were captains who could, and sometimes did, lash the flesh off the seaman's back for a word or a look of mutiny; there were sharks ashore and there was the enemy afloat. Yet nothing, not the warnings of the experienced or the history of terrible shipwrecks, or the certain knowledge of these things, could keep the young sailor ashore or make him prefer the counter to the deck.

James Cook was such a boy. He heard these voices and had these visions. Perhaps among the fisher-folk of the Staithes there may have been one or two who had sailed through the Strait le Maire and up the coast of Chile and Peru and even beyond and north of the Island of California, escaping from the Spanish fleet and boldly tackling the biggest and strongest Spanish ship, and so across the great Pacific Ocean, on the parallel of latitude 13° N., to the Isle of Guam, whence, through friendly seas and round the Cape of Good Hope, home. There came a time when he could resist no longer, and he fled.

Legends have grown up around this Hejira, from which Cook's life should be dated. It is said that he quarrelled with his master; it is said that he demanded to have his articles broken; it is further said that, in order to pay for a conveyance from the Staithes to Whitby, he stole a shilling from the till. The preservation of the till itself, which was shown until quite recently, has always been considered sufficient proof of this story of the stolen shilling. True it is that on the spot certain of the oldest inhabitants endeavour to soften down the story, to remove from it the more tragic elements, which really constitute its strength, and lend it a moral, by alleging that James Cook did not steal a shilling, but that he exchanged an old for a new shilling, by which his master was in no way injured. Now the mute evidence of the till in no way supports this explanation. It says plainly, "Either a shilling was stolen from me, or it was not. Looking into the receptacles and the depths of me, what do you think?

About the breaking of the articles, the boy's parents were fifteen miles away, and practically inaccessible: articles of apprenticeship were not broken without a great deal of trouble and some expense; boys who want to go to sea have never troubled themselves about legal formalities; they run away. Robinson Crusoe, the leading case, ran away. James Cook ran away; he tied up his belongings, one shirt and a jack-knife, in his only handkerchief, stole out of the house one summer morning at daybreak, looked across the bay for a moment, marked how the rising sun gilded the sails of the coaster a mile out at sea, looked regretfully at the row of boats lying on the beach or anchored in the harbour, and then strode away along the narrow street of the town, where all were asleep except himself.

And as to that conveyance to Whitby, considering that the distance is no more than nine or ten miles, or perhaps a little more by way of the cliff; that there was then no road, except a bridle-path, between any of the villages along that coast; that there were then no carts, carriages, or vehicles of any kind running between Whitby and the Staithes; and that he was a stout and sturdy lad, we may without difficulty acknowledge that he did the little journey on foot, and that if he took that shilling at all, which a biographer who loves his hero may be permitted to doubt, it was to provide himself with food until he should get what he wanted, a ship.

This, one feels quite certain, is the exact truth. But in order to make the thing perfectly clear, let me borrow a page from the *Book of the Things Forgotten*, a work too generally neglected by the historian.

On Monday morning, the 5th July 1742, Mr. Sanderson, grocer and draper, awoke somewhat later than usual; he knew it was later because he heard the washing of the waves upon the Staithe; the tide was up; he remembered that the high tide was due at six o'clock that morning, men who live by the sea always know the time of day by the tide, and the time when high tide and low tide are due. He got out of bed, therefore, being reminded, at the same time, by a certain heaviness of head, that he had taken more beer than is needful for man's refreshment at the *Cod and Lobster* the night before.

Then he dressed leisurely, and descended the narrow stair into his shop. He found, to his astonishment, that the place was still closed, and, as the sunshine streaming through the upper holes of the shutters showed, that the floor was unswept and nothing set out upon the counter. Mr. Sanderson had his misgivings, taught by past experience. He said nothing; he crept with silence and great caution to the corner where stood the instrument with which he daily admonished his apprentice, grasped it and stole to the counter under which the boy made his bed at night, intent on giving him a lesson, short and practical, on the duty of early rising, one, he thought, that should leave a lasting impression. There was no boy. The blanket was thrown back, the sacking on which he lay was crumpled up: the boy had left his bed. Mr. Sanderson laid down the stick and tried the door; it was unbolted and unlocked: the boy had therefore gone. Then Mr. Sanderson sighed and replaced the cane in its corner. It would wait for the next apprentice, for this one had run away and gone to sea. He made no inquiries, and had no doubts. All the boys who were indentured to this good man ran away and went to sea. He could not keep them, though he flogged them every day; they would go to sea, where the floggings were more frequent and more various, ranging from the dread cat with nine tails to the handy rope's end. They would go James Cook had only followed the others. He remembered, now that it was too late, certain symptoms which should have warned him, a new restlessness in the boy, a careless weighing of the brown sugar, a lavish rendering of a yard of Welsh flannel, and a certain wistful look in his eyes whenever he could steal to the door and gaze upon the water. Well, he had gone to sea; another apprentice must be found; perhaps James would be wrecked and cast away, or he might fall overboard, or the ship might founder, or he might get tired of the sea life, and, being unfitted for a landsman's drudgery, turn vagabond, highwayman, footpad, and so get hanged ; or he might become a steady and useful sailor, and come back to give an account of himself.

With these thoughts he opened the till. It was empty. He remembered leaving a bright shilling in it on Saturday evening. It was empty. The young villain, he had robbed the till. He took it in his hand and went to the door; hard by were the coble men leaning against the posts.

"Men," said Mr. Sanderson, "ha' ye seen James Cook? He's run away and robbed the till of a shilling."

Up spoke a gray-haired mariner.

"Robbed t' till, man? Thou robbed it thysel' last night to pay tha reckonin'. Art too drunk yet to mind gaein' oot for t' money?"

Mr. Sanderson retired with his empty till. But the word had been spoken, and it was spread abroad in the Staithes, and contradicted, and again reported, that James Cook had not only run away to sea but had robbed the till of a new shilling. For there is a sticking quality about a

11

lie, particularly a lie which degrades, if it is believed; and to this day … but the rest we know.

The good man took another apprentice, and yet another, and another. They all ran away and went to sea, except one, who was preparing to go too when a putrid fever seized him, caused by the stinking fish. He departed, too, but not in the same way, and now lies buried in Hinderwell churchyard, under a grassy mound, and is forgotten. The shop, as has been already stated, stands no longer. The *Cod and Lobster*, then the first house in the row under the south cliff, is now the only house left. For a few years after the flight of James Cook there arose one night a mighty storm of wind and rain; the waves came rolling in from the north, the tide ran over the Staithes and flooded the lower part of the town. The people in this row of houses had to fly for their lives, and one by one the buildings fell and were washed away before the tide went down.

All but the old tavern, which still stands to show the kind of hostelry which was the fisherman's house of resort in the year 1740 or thereabouts. The respectable Sanderson saved his effects and furniture, and his till. The shop was reopened in a house higher up; the house still stands, but the shop is closed. When Mr. Sanderson at length concluded his pilgrimage, one Turner took it over in his place, Sanderson having no sons, or, which is possible, all Sanderson's sons having run away and gone to sea. Turner in due course gave place to one Row, who is also now gone, and the shop is closed. The till has disappeared, and will no longer bear evidence, the dumb, helpless thing, to an invention. Perhaps it has been acquired by the Library of the Royal Geographical Society, or it may be among the treasures of the Royal Society. I have looked for it in the Museum of Whitby, but it is not there.

James Cook came no more to the Staithes. The people, however, heard of him. He was seen at Whitby between voyages. Ten years or so later the news came that he had been pressed into the king's navy. And one day, twenty years and more after he had run away, the news came to this little port that Lieutenant Cook, nothing less, if you please, than Lieutenant, had sailed away in command of a king's ship, bound for the Pacific Ocean, whither men go to fight the Spaniard. Never before, in the memory of man, had officer of the Royal Navy come from the Staithes. Captains of fishing smacks, even of colliers, but Lieutenants in the Royal Navy? Never.

"Why, James Cook was my apprentice!" said Mr. Sanderson, now old and shaken in his memory. "He ran away and went to sea, and he robbed the till; ay, he took a new shilling out of the till. This very till it was, a new shilling. Though they did say, "But here his memory failed him.

They cherish the memory of James Cook's boyhood all over Cleveland. The strangers who visit the Staithes from Whitby or from Saltburn are told where was the house in which Cook served part of an apprenticeship. At Marton, where the great sailor was born, there is a school named after him. At Great Ayton they show the house built by his father, after the great sailor had left the place, and the schoolhouse, rebuilt after the great sailor had gone away. There is a monument to his memory erected upon a hill near Ayton for all the world to see; and at Whitby, in the museum, they have his portrait, and a relic or two from the *Endeavour*, and a collection of South Sea arms, dresses, and implements, which, though presented by various donors, are accepted by the visitor as placed there in honour of Captain Cook, and if you make your way to the little street where he was articled, half a dozen of the people run forth instantly to point out the house.

CHAPTER II

BEFORE THE MAST

THE boy, as the book above quoted goes on to explain, turned to the southward when he reached the top of the cliff, and walked across the fields through Hinderwell churchyard, to the road which, in the year 1742, was only a cross country track, and not a made road at all, leading to the village of Lythe. Here he struck into the way along the cliff made by those who searched for jet and those who worked in the alum trade, and so walked into Whitby, which he reached before the events already narrated, concerned with the awaking of Mr. Sanderson, happened. It was not yet six o'clock when he stood upon the west cliff, on which there was not a single house, and looked down upon the town below.

He saw a closely built populous place, the houses stuck together as if to prevent each other from falling from the steep sides of the cliff into the port itself. There was no street on the west side except the Staithe itself, the long quay, behind which the houses began; narrow courts with stone steps led up between the lower houses to those above; the roofs were of bright red tiles; the coal smoke hung over the town; there was an inner port connected with the outer by a swing bridge; already the town was astir; the cobles and the smacks had come in and were unloading their cargo; a sale was going on loud and noisy; the beadle was bawling the loss of a mare, lost, stolen, or strayed, and ringing his bell; with many "yeo hoes" they were warping a ship out of harbour; from the dockyard beyond the inner port there came the beating of a hundred hammers, wielded by those who built the sturdy Whitby craft; the children played about the quay, sliding up and down the ropes, and looking at the casks filled with fish to be sent up country and sold; the carts stood ready of those who were waiting to carry the fish about the farms and villages; Whitby was awake, arid in the full swing of work.

It was then, as now, a busy and important place; it had a population of nearly ten thousand; many ships were built there; it furnished ships and crews for the coal trade along the coast; the Whitby ships traded with Norway, Sweden, Hamburg, Bremen, Dantzig, and St. Petersburg; a large part of the Baltic trade was in the hands of Whitby; her merchants and shipowners were wealthy and responsible persons; Whitby sent out whalers; Whitby sent to London iron, stone, alum, and jet; at Whitby there were made ropes, sails, blocks, yards, and all kinds of gear wanted for ships; and Whitby was the centre of a great fishery.

In those days it had but one church, the old church on the east cliff, up the long flight of two hundred steps. It was so crowded on Sunday morning that they had already pulled down the north aisle and built up the large square structure which still stands; they had also already begun the construction of the galleries, which are stuck all about the church wherever one can be placed; they had also already squared off the roof, put in the skylights, and modernised the windows. The name of the place was by some written Whitebay; it is so spelt on the tombstone of a certain minister of the parish who died in the beginning of the century; but this was pedantic. The old name of the town, Streoneshalh, has long been forgotten, which is a thousand pities; in the same way the old name of the little hamlet three miles north, Thordisa, has been clean forgotten, and changed into East Row, which is indeed a drop.

The boy saw the church on the east cliff, and behind it the ruins of St. Hilda's abbey church, in his day the central tower was still standing; he saw one ship going out of harbour, and another ship taking her cargo on board. He walked quickly down the west cliff to the quay, boarded the ship, and doffed his cap to the mate.

Under the east cliff there is nestled the oldest part of Whitby town; here is the old town hall, built upon a great central pillar, thicker than those of Durham Cathedral, with a pillar of more slender diameter for each of the corners. Here are two narrow streets running parallel with the cliff, and half a dozen courts running up the lower slope before the cliff begins. Under the town hall is the market; as you see it to-day, so James Cook saw it that day when he walked in from Staithes: pigs and sheep, poultry, fruit, and vegetables are sold in this market. For fish you can go to the quay on the other side. Many of the houses in this part of the town have got the date of their erection over the doors; one is dated 1704, another 1688, and so on; by far the greater part of them are more than a hundred years old. In the lower of the two streets, courts nearly as narrow as the Yarmouth passages run down to the water's edge, or to houses built overhanging the water. Some of these are old taverns; they have, built outside, broad wooden galleries or verandahs, with green railings, and steps to the water, where the captains or mates of the colliers could sit with a pipe and a cool tankard, and gossip away the time between dinner and supper, looking out to sea the while between the cliffs. When the sailor is not afloat he loves to sit where he can gaze upon a harbour and ships and the blue water outside. At the *Raffled Anchor*, for instance, even a sluggish imagination can easily discern James Cook himself, in his rough sea dress and tarred hands, sitting among his friends and shipmates, himself already having gained the quarterdeck. He is a silent young man; he refuses not his drink, but he does not sing and bluster; indeed, the Whitby mariners were ever a quiet and God-fearing folk, though in the matter of drink, but were they worse than the landsmen? A picture of Whitby of this date tells little that one who knows the place cannot discover on the spot; the reconstruction of the town of 1742 needs but the knocking down of the modern part and of a few shop fronts and recent structures. The build of the Whitby ship, in the picture one is lying in the inner harbour, has been little modified. She is round in the bow, broad and square in the stern; her lines are laid for room rather than for speed; her length is about three times her breadth. In the picture, just as now, the houses cluster at the foot of the east cliff, the dockyard is in full activity, the port is full of bustle and business.

The *Book of Things Forgotten* narrates that the ship in which Cook offered his services was ready for sea; that he was taken on board as ship's boy, and proved himself, during the voyage to London port and home, a lad of quick parts and great activity, insomuch that the rope's end was seldom required to start him, and the mate, though a choleric person, found it unnecessary to cuff the boy unless he was actually within reach. Further, that this officer interested himself, being of a generous and humane disposition, in the boy, and advised him to get bound to the owners of the ship for a term of years, holding out his own remarkable rise from the position of apprentice to be mate or first lieutenant of the collier. To this rank, he said, the boy might himself reasonably and even laudably aspire, though it was given to few to reach so dizzy an elevation. In short, he persuaded the boy for his own good.

The owners of the ship were two Quaker merchants, brothers, named John and Henry Walker. They lived together, and had their office in the narrow street now named Chapel Lane, but then a continuation of Sandgate. Their house, now converted into two, still stands, a plain, Quaker like house. These worthy gentlemen received the lad as their apprentice, bound to them for seven, or, as some say, for nine years, presumably with the consent of his father, and perhaps, though this is improbable, after the former articles with Mr. Sanderson had been torn up and annulled.

The period which follows is perfectly dark and obscure; nor is it possible to ascertain much which may be relied upon as to the boy's work between the years 1742 and 1755. He remained in the service of the two Quakers; it is commonly assumed that he spent the whole time on board a collier trading up and down the coast. This, however, is not the case, because we find him in later years telling Mr. Forster on his second voyage of his voyages to Norway. I am certain that he never went whaling, because his own remarks on the subject of the Antarctic ice do not show any experience of ice, nor does he use the whaler's language in speaking of the various kinds of ice encountered by those who sail off the coasts of Greenland and Labrador. He says, indeed, on his first meeting with the southern ice: "I had two men on board that had been in the Greenland trade; the one of them in a ship that lay nine weeks, and the other in one that lay six weeks fast in this kind of ice, which they called packed ice." Therefore he was never himself in the Greenland trade, nor was he ever in the Russian trade, or he would have shown some knowledge of the Russians when he afterwards met them in Behring's Straits. Even the *Book of Things Forgotten* can tell nothing more about this period. He began it as an apprentice, he ended it as mate. That is all. As regards the life led on board the merchant ship, it seems to have been much the same as that in the Royal Navy; the men were perhaps knocked about more and flogged less; there was little discipline, but much swearing, cuffing, and, in case of mutiny, the officers had to be ready to fell the mutineers with the first weapon that came handy, a marline-spike, a cutlass, or anything. As for the rations and general living, I suppose they were much the same on a merchantman as on a king's ship, and we shall presently see how the men lived in the Royal Navy in the middle of the eighteenth century. As for the things that the boy would learn, they would be all summed up under the head of practical seamanship; he would learn first all the parts of a ship and her rigging; the sails, the running and the standing gear, and how to use them; he would learn how to sail a ship, how to steer her, how to save her in time of storm and danger ; in the thirteen years that he worked for the Quaker brothers, there was plenty of time to acquire a thorough knowledge of seamanship. This period, indeed, proved the foundation of the lad's fortune; he became a sailor. But for book learning I cannot understand how he could acquire any. The captain and the mate would have one or two of the handbooks used by all sailors; readers of this series have heard from Mr. Clark Russell, in his *Life of Dampier*, of a sailor's *Waggoner*; there was also the sailor's *Vade Mecum*, containing all kinds of practical rules and information. Apart from such books, I think there could have been nothing to help the boy. He preserved, however, the thirst for reading first implanted in him by Mistress Walker at Marton; a boy with an active and curious mind never loses that thirst.

It is also reasonable to suppose, since he was promoted and became mate of his vessel, that his conduct and ability proved satisfactory to his employers; he would probably have received the command of a ship but for the accident which changed the whole current of his life, and enabled him to achieve the glory that belongs to the great navigators of the world.

Early in the year 1755, though the country was then nominally at peace with France, it was felt necessary for the protection of the colonies to send a fleet to the American station, with orders to attack any French squadron which might be found in those waters, where it was assumed that they could be sailing with none other than hostile intentions. These instructions were given openly, and were communicated to the French Court by the ambassador. The king replied that the firing of the first shot would be regarded as a declaration of war.

That shot was fired on the 6th of June, but war was not formally declared before May 17th in the following year. This was the last struggle by which Great Britain, at the expense of millions of money and lives sacrificed by thousands, succeeded in freeing her colonies from the European Powers. At the close of the war in 1762, the whole of Canada, the islands of St. John and Cape Breton, Louisiana east of the Mississippi, the free navigation of that river, and the province of Florida, had been acquired for Great Britain. France retained nothing except the two islets of St. Pierre and Miquelon, which she still keeps. Unhappily, the peace also allowed her the right of fishing on the banks of Newfoundland, which was withdrawn from Spain. This peace was signed in 1763. Only twelve years later our grateful colonists took advantage of the expulsion of French and Spaniards to throw off their allegiance to the British Crown, without accepting any part of the burdens laid upon the mother country in her long struggle for their protection.

The imminent war caused a press, both hot and heavy, in every part of the United Kingdom. Nowhere was it so hot as in the port of London, with its thousand ships and its tens of thousands of sailors. At this moment Cook's vessel, the *Free Love* of Whitby, was lying in the river. Although he was now a mate on board, he was by no means free of the pressgang, nor would his position on board a collier help him to any rating on board a man-of-war above that of able seaman. There was a way, however, better than that of being pressed: it was to enter as a volunteer. It must be remembered that the service was not then governed by the same rigid rules as now prevail. A man might, and sometimes did, obtain a commission in the navy without going through the preliminary and lower ranks. The branch in which a man with a practical knowledge of seamanship might reasonably hope to rise was that of master's mate first and master afterwards. Also, it was not the branch in which he would have to encounter aristocratic influence and favouritism. Young gentlemen who entered the navy had no desire to become masters. Those who went into this line were practical sailors, men as tough and often as rough as the common seamen, who lived, when they were at home, at Wapping, Poplar, Shadwell, and Stepping, if they belonged to the port of London; or at Point, Gosport, and certain streets outside the dockyard walls at Portsmouth if they belonged to that town. Cook, at that time twenty-seven years of age, resolved that he would not be a pressed man. He would enter as a volunteer. Accordingly he repaired to a rendezvous at Wapping, where he entered as an able seaman on board the *Eagle*, sixty guns, Captain John Earner. This was in May 1755. In October of the same year Captain (afterwards Sir Hugh) Palliser was appointed captain.

CHAPTER III

IN THE ROYAL NAVY

BETWEEN May 1755 and May 1759 is a period of four years. It is the second blank space in Cook's life. Nobody has attempted to fill up this blank. He was with Palliser on board the *Eagle*. The *Eagle* formed part of the American fleet. As it is very well known that Captain Palliser took an active share in whatever was going, we may reasonably conclude that Cook was also present in many of the actions of the time. The war began, as usual, badly. Boscawen was sent out to intercept the French fleet and failed, General Braddock was defeated and slain. On the other hand, our cruisers and privateers almost annihilated the French trade in the West Indies. As many as eight thousand French prisoners, with three hundred merchant ships, were captured in those seas. Admiral Holborne was sent out with a powerful fleet to co-operate with Lord Loudon in the reduction of Canada, but nothing was done. In 1758, however, Palliser was at the taking of Louisburg and the reduction of the whole island of Cape Breton. In this action five French frigates were taken and five destroyed. The French islands of Guadaloupe, Descada, and Marie Galante were taken. In 1759 the *Eagle* returned to England.

This is the brief record of those four years. What share Cook had in these actions does not appear. But when fighting begins, no one on board can avoid his share of the danger at least. It is certain that from the outset Cook could never have been confounded with the ordinary able seaman, nothing is more clear than the profound ignorance and the brutality of the common sailor of the eighteenth century. He had no forethought, he was childishly dependent on his superior officers. He had, it is true, the common virtues of discipline, obedience, endurance, and bull-dog courage; but that was all. He drank as much as he could get; he threw away his money; he lived for the day. When, for instance, the *Resolution* sailed out of the Arctic Ocean, we read that the sailors put off their warm clothes and began kicking them about decks, as if they would never experience any more cold. The officers, to save the things, collected them and laid them by in casks.

A man who understood the art of navigation could not remain a common sailor. In the naval records of the time one reads once, and once only, of such a man. He was on board Sir Cloudesley Shovel's ship, the *Association*. This wonderful person calculated the course of the ship, he discovered that the officers were out in their reckoning, he knew that they were dangerously near the Scilly rocks; he said so. They hanged him for mutiny; and the next day the ship ran upon these rocks, and behold! they were all dead men.

What probably happened was this: On the *Discovery* that there was on board an able seaman, a volunteer, who understood the art of navigation, the man would have been picked out and kept on deck engaged in navigating the ship. He would have been told off to help in the duties of the master. One solitary scrap of paper remains in Cook's handwriting which belongs to this period. It is cut out of a book, it is dated "Wednesday, Nov. 3rd, 1756," and it contains certain calculations, apparently in navigation. It is perhaps a rough or draft logbook. Therefore, a year after his volunteering, Cook was no longer a common sailor, but doing the work of the master's branch. Was he promoted to the acting rank of master's mate?

It seems impossible to answer this question. The single fact remains that on the ship's return, Captain Palliser received a letter from Mr. Osbaldiston, M.P. for Scarborough, asking if something could be done for James Cook, volunteer on board his ship. Why should Mr. Osbaldiston interfere in his behalf? Fountain Wentworth Osbaldiston was the fourth son of an Osbaldiston of Hunmanby, near Filey. They were a very considerable family, lords of Havercroft. There were five sons, two of them successively members for Scarborough; one was Bishop of London. All died without issue. It is a long journey from Great Ayton to Hunmanby, but we may fairly suppose that it was at the request of Mr. Skottowe that the letter was written. However that may be, Palliser gave his support to Cook, and he was raised to the rank of master, and appointed to the *Grampus*. When it was found that the former master of the *Grampus* had returned to his ship, Cook's appointment was transferred to the *Garland*. It was discovered that the Garland had already sailed. Cook was then appointed to the *Mercury*. So far, then, this young man had done pretty well. To rise from a collier's apprentice to be master, not master's mate, but full master, on board a king's ship by the age of thirty must be considered creditable indeed. No doubt at the time Cook thought he had touched the highest point.

We may now consider how far advanced he was at this time in scientific attainment. His practical seamanship recommended him for promotion. What was it that recommended him for the services he was immediately to perform? Kippis tells the story in words which there is no need to alter.

The destination of the *Mercury* was to North America, where she joined the fleet under the command of Sir Charles Saunders, which, in conjunction with the land forces under General Wolfe, was engaged in the famous siege of Quebec. During that siege a dangerous and difficult service was necessary to be performed. This was to take the soundings in the channel of the river St. Lawrence, between the island of Orleans and the north shore, directly in the front of the French fortified camp at Montmorency and Beauport, in order to enable the admiral to place ships against the enemy's batteries, and to cover our army in a general attack which the heroic Wolfe intended to make on the camp. Captain Palliser, in consequence of his acquaintance with Mr. Cook's sagacity and *Resolution*, recommended him to the service, and he performed it in the most complete manner. In this business he was employed during the night time for several nights together. At length he was discovered by the enemy, who collected a great number of Indians and canoes in a wood near the waterside, which were launched in the night for the purpose of surrounding him and cutting him off. On this occasion he had a very narrow escape. He was obliged to run for it, and pushed on shore on the island of Orleans, near the guard of the English hospital. Some of the Indians entered at the stern of the boat as Mr. Cook leaped out at the bow; and the boat, which was a barge belonging to one of the ships of war, was carried away in triumph. However, he furnished the admiral with as correct and complete a draught of the channel and soundings as could have been made after our countrymen were in possession of Quebec. Sir Hugh Palliser has good reason to believe that before this time Mr. Cook had scarcely ever used a pencil, and that he knew nothing of drawing. But such was his capacity that he speedily made himself master of every object to which he applied his attention.

Another important service was performed by Mr. Cook while the fleet continued in the river St. Lawrence. The navigation of that river is exceedingly difficult and hazardous. It was particularly so to the English, who were then in a great measure strangers to this part of North America, and who had no chart on the correctness of which they could depend. It was, therefore, ordered by the admiral that Mr. Cook should be employed to survey those parts of the river below Quebec which navigators had experienced to be attended with peculiar difficulty and danger, and he executed the business with the same diligence and skill of which he had already afforded so happy a specimen. When he had finished the undertaking, his chart of the river St. Lawrence was published, with soundings and directions for sailing in that river. Of the accuracy and utility of this chart it is sufficient to say that it hath never since been found necessary to publish any other. One which has appeared in France is only a copy of the author's on a reduced scale.

Such were the services which he performed within a few weeks after his appointment as master. It is clear that such work would never have been entrusted to a young man who possessed no other qualifications than the knowledge of handling a ship. One does not generally step all at once from the rank of able seaman to the preparation of a most important chart and the examination of a difficult seaway. Nor were Cook's previous services the only reason why he should be selected from all the officers of the fleet for the important duty. Special knowledge, as well as special aptitude, must have been understood.

These considerations prove that he already possessed special knowledge. How he acquired it, by whose assistance, who lent him books, how he found time or opportunity, it is impossible to learn. Most of this knowledge must have been learned during the four years in the Royal Navy. It must, however, be noted that there is no other case on record in which a sailor boy starting in the very lowest place with the humblest origin and the very smallest outfit of learning, has so far succeeded as to be promoted at thirty to the rank of master in the king's navy, and immediately afterwards to be selected for the performance of a piece of work requiring great technical knowledge, and one would think, considerable experience.

As for his personal appearance, several portraits remain of him. The best seems to be that by Webber, the artist of his third voyage. Every biography ought, at that point when the keynote of the character is struck, to establish clearly in the mind of the reader the true effigies of the man. One is not interested in the personal appearance of James Cook, mate of a collier; but when James Cook has become a master in the Royal Navy, when the really important step in his career has been taken in the execution of special service by special appointment, it is time that we should learn what manner of man he was to those who only looked upon him. We know a man when we have seen him, when we have spoken with him or heard him speak, when we have read his books or his letters, and when we know what he has done. Cook's voice is not often heard; for the most part others speak for him and of him; but his portrait remains.

He was, to begin with, over six feet high, thin and spare; his head was small; his forehead was broad; his hair was of a dark brown, rolled back and tied behind in the fashion of the time; his nose was long and straight; his nostrils clear and finely cut; his cheekbones were high, a feature which illustrated his Scotch descent; his eyes were brown and small, but well set, quick, and piercing; his eyebrows were large and bushy; his chin was round and full; his mouth firmly set; his face long. It is an austere face, but striking. One thinks, perhaps wrongly, that without having been told whose face this is, in the portrait, we might know it as the face of a man remarkable for patience, *Resolution,* perseverance, and indomitable courage. The portraits of naval worthies are sometimes disappointing, the faces of some gallant admirals have even, if one may respectfully use the word, a fatuous expression, no doubt the fault of the rascal painter. That of James Cook satisfies. It is a face worthy of the navigator. Such was the appearance of the man: tall, thin, grave, even austere. As for his personal habits, he was, as all agree, of robust constitution, inured to labour, and capable of undergoing the severest hardships. Every north-easterly gale that buffeted the collier's boy in the German Ocean, every night spent in battling with the winter gales between Newcastle and the port of London, helped to build up this strength and endurance. He was able to eat without difficulty the coarsest and the most ungrateful food, on what luxuries are even the mates of a collier nourished? "Great was the indifference with which he submitted to every kind of self-denial." A man who felt no hardships, who desired no better fare than was served out to his men, who looked on rough weather as the chief part of life, who was never sick, and never tired, where was there his like?

And a man who never rested: he was always at work. "During his long and tedious voyages," writes Captain King after his death, "his eagerness and activity were never in the least degree abated. No incidental temptation would detain him for a moment; even those intervals of recreation which sometimes unavoidably occurred, and were looked for by us with a longing that persons who have experienced the fatigues of service will readily excuse, were submitted to by him with a certain impatience whenever they could not be employed in making a further provision for the more effectual prosecution of his designs."

When we have read so far we are not surprised to hear that he was a man of a hasty temper and liable to passion. A man who was never tired, never wanting to sit down and rest, impatient of enforced leisure, careless about luxuries, incessantly at work, how should he be anything but hasty and passionate when he found his plans obstructed by the weakness or the laziness of men?

All that follows will illustrate the fidelity of this portrait. The man commanded unbounded respect, fear, obedience, and confidence from his crew. What his private and intimate friends said and thought of him is unknown to us. Beneath the austere commander there was, it is admitted by all, a kindly and human heart. We must look for proof to the journals of his voyages, because there does not survive, to my knowledge, a single letter from him, or a single word from a personal friend.

His private life, how he lived and talked at home and among his old friends and cronies, is almost as much lost to us as the private life of Shakespeare. Certainly he had some friends, it is most likely that he had very few. For, if we consider, the course of his life from the age of twenty-seven was not such as to continue the old friendships. The rude sailors among whom his boyhood was passed, the rough officers of the merchant service among whom he spent his early manhood, those people could hardly have anything more in common with the most scientific officer in His Majesty's Navy. James Cook, master, occupied a rank very far above that of many of his former associates. When one rises in the world it is necessary to abandon many old acquaintances; those left behind are apt to complain, but they forget the great gulf that success and promotion make between old acquaintances. Most of Cook's old shipmates were still before the mast; the rest were still navigating merchant vessels, for the most part looking on a warm room in a Whitby tavern, with a pipe and a glass of punch, as the only occupation worthy of a sensible man's time ashore. With such as these what had Cook to do? Nor, indeed, would he readily make friends in the navy, except with those of his superior officers who discovered his worth and knew how to value his qualities. He had few private friends; if there had been many, legends would have survived from some; there would have been old men proud to tell how Captain Cook, the great captain, was an old friend; how he would come and talk during the brief visits home; what things he brought them from abroad, a conch from Tahiti, a piece of coral from New Caledonia, a tomahawk from New Zealand. Long after life is over for every great man there survive such memories, for they have had their private friends; but Cook had no friends, and no such memories are gathered round his name. It is little more than a hundred years since Cook was killed; men are living still who might have talked with such old friends of Cook. Why, I myself, I who write this book, have talked with a man who was a page to Marie Antoinette; I myself, but little beyond the tenth lustrum, have talked with one who was a drummer-boy to Henri Larochejaquelin; I have talked with those who fought at Copenhagen, the Nile, and Trafalgar ; and had Captain Cook left private and personal friends, I might have talked with their sons, and heard what things the great man had said, because their memory would have been cherished in the family. Again, some men are so self-reliant, and some are so constantly absorbed in their work, that they want none of the sympathies and the supports of friendship. When Cook speaks of friends he means patrons. I cannot believe that there were officers of the same rank with himself with whom he could talk of the social life of which he knew so little; nor can I believe that there were cronies with whom he would sit in his front garden in the Mile End Road, a cool tankard between them and a pipe of tobacco in their hands, to gossip away the afternoon, and while the hours from dinner to supper. And I cannot, further, believe that any old intimacies, had there been any, with the Whitby shipmates were still maintained. Therefore I think that Cook had very few private friends.

The post of master, which lasted until thirty years ago, when it was followed by that of navigating lieutenant, now also abolished, was the survival of the sixteenth and seventeenth century practice of appointing as captain a soldier who had no knowledge of navigation, but was to command the fighting. The duties of the master, as laid down in the sailor's *Vade Mecum* of the year 1780, were briefly: To navigate the ship under the directions of her superior officer, to see that the logbook was kept, to inspect all stores and provisions, to stow the hold, trim the ship, take care of the ballast, to observe coasts, shoals, and rocks, and to sign vouchers and accounts. In other words, he was the chief executive officer on board. His scale of pay shows the importance of his post. It varied from £4 a month on board a Sixth Rate to £9 : 2s. a month on a First Rate. As the pay of a lieutenant did not exceed £7 a month on a First Rate, the master was thought of more importance than a lieutenant. The surgeon was paid £5 a month; the captain eight guineas a month on a Sixth Rate and £28 on a First Rate. Besides their pay the officers were entitled to the same rations as the men, and though they commuted the rations and brought on board their own stores, it is evident from the low rate of pay that for the most part the officers must have fared very little better than the men. This, indeed, is abundantly clear from the pages of Smollett. The full weekly allowance of provisions for every man was as follows. This was to be reckoned apart from fresh fish, which was ordered to be distributed as caught without any reduction in the regular allowance. On the whole, comparing it with the modern allowance, Jack of the last century seems to have been better off than Jack of the present.

Seven pounds of biscuit.	One quart of pease.
Seven gallons of beer.	Three pints of oatmeal.
Two pounds of pork.	Six ounces of butter.
Four pounds of beef.	Twelve ounces of cheese.

On comparing the daily allowance of the last with that of the present century we have

THEN	NOW
One pound of biscuit.	One pound and a quarter of biscuit, or one pound and a half of bread.
One gallon of beer.	One ounce cocoa, one-quarter ounce tea, two ounces sugar, half gill rum.
Six-sevenths of a pound of meat.	One pound of meat.
One-seventh of a quart of pease.	Half a pound of vegetables.
Three-sevenths of a peck of oatmeal.	
Six-sevenths of an ounce of butter.	No oatmeal, no butter and no cheese.
One and five-sevenths of an ounce of cheese.	

As regards water, one ton of water was allowed for every hundred men per month. There were no rations of rum, but the regulations provided that on foreign voyages, where beer could not be procured, the men might have half a pint of rum, brandy, or arrack in lieu of beer. As yet no tea, coffee, or cocoa was served out to the sailors. The national drink, the drink of the people, was beer; they drank beer for breakfast, beer for dinner, beer for supper, and beer at all other times when they could get it. A gallon of beer, four quarts or eight pints, is, it must be confessed, a plentiful allowance, an affectionate and kindly allowance, for the daily drink; its substitute, when there was no beer, of half a pint of rum or brandy would be more than most of us moderns would care to take in the day, however much diluted. No tobacco was served out; but the purser could sell it to the men "in some public place," and in quantities not exceeding two pounds for any one man in one month. Half a pound of tobacco a week, over one ounce a day is a liberal allowance. Jack, no doubt, already practised afloat the delectable and delicate habit of chewing, but as he was only allowed tobacco when off duty, he must have found it difficult to get through an ounce a day. That they did smoke pipes is certain from the general instructions in the duties of a lieutenant that he is not to permit smoking between decks. As for the use of wine by the officers, nothing is said. The captain's table seems to have been always provided with Madeira, a favourite wine at sea; that of the officers would be perhaps supplied from their own stores as long as these held out; but it must be remembered that very few of the officers were men of private fortunes, and even a lieutenant's pay would not stand the daily exhibition of Madeira. I can find no allusion to the drinking of tea or coffee in Cook's Voyages either as a daily practice or an exceptional thing. But they had some vessels on board which they could use as teapots, because they are mentioned by name when the spruce tea brewed in Dusky Bay is described. Certainly Captain Cook was not brought up on tea, coffee, or chocolate.

In September of the same year Cook was transferred from the *Mercury* to the *Northumberland*, a first-rate man-of-war, the Admiral's ship. They wintered at Halifax; during the winter Cook is said to have first begun the study of geometry, mathematics, and astronomy. The amount of mathematics required for the practice of marine surveying, taking observations, making charts, calculating latitudes and longitudes, is not very considerable; but that a man should actually begin the study of mathematics after thirty, and after performing surveys and making charts, can hardly be believed. That Cook spent a laborious winter working at those branches of mathematical science which are concerned with navigation, that he advanced himself considerably, and that he brought a clear head and a strong will to the work, may be and must be believed.

The *Northumberland* returned to England in the autumn of 1762, and on December 21st of that year Cook was married. The following is the entry in the parish register of St. Margaret's, Barking, Essex.

James Cook of y Parish of St. Paul, Shadwell, in y county of Middlesex, Bachelor, and Elizabeth Batts of y Parish of Barking in y county of Essex, Spinster, were married in this church by y Archbishop of Canterbury's licence this 21st day of December one thousand seven hundred and sixty-two.

By GEORGE DOWNING,

Vicar of Little Wakering, Essex.

The signatures follow with those of the witnesses.

I am indebted to the Rev. Canon Bennett of Shrewton, Wilts, for information respecting Elizabeth Batts which no one else now possesses. She belonged to a highly respectable middle-class family, connected with various manufactures and industries. Charles Smith, her grandfather, was a currier, carrying on business in Bermondsey. His son Charles was a shipping agent in the Customhouse. His daughter Mary married, first, one John Batts, who was in business at Wapping; and secondly, John Blackburn, in business at Shadwell. Mrs. Cook's first cousin, Charles Smith, became a very successful manufacturer of watches and clocks. His house and factory were in Bunhill Row. His eldest son Isaac, who accompanied Captain Cook in his first and second voyages, subsequently retired with the rank of admiral. His second son Charles, of Merton Abbey, possessed considerable property in Merton and elsewhere. For Cook to marry into so substantial and respectable a family marks a social lift corresponding to his promotion in the navy. There is more to say about this lady later on. Meantime, my authority, who remembers her perfectly well, she lived to a very advanced age, bears testimony to the full that her appearance in age showed how singularly beautiful she must have been in youth, that her manners were good and full of dignity, and that she was well educated. She loved to tell how on the day of her wedding she walked with Mr. Cook across the meadows to the church. Therefore she was living outside the town of Barking. As her grandfather came originally from Essex, she was probably staying with relations. The newly married pair went to live in Shadwell, where Mrs. Cook's mother, then Mrs. Blackburn, resided. Afterwards they removed to the Mile End Road.

Cook was now thirty-four years of age. The spells of domestic felicity which he was destined to enjoy were both short and few. Four months after his marriage his services were applied for by Captain Graves, who had obtained a grant for the survey of Newfoundland. Accordingly, in April 1763, he went out and surveyed the islands of Miquelon and St. Pierre, which had been ceded to the French by the Treaty of Peace, and were about to be occupied by them.

This job finished, he returned to England. Early in 1764, however, his constant friend and patron, Sir Hugh Palliser, having been appointed Governor and Commodore of Newfoundland and Labrador, offered Cook an appointment as marine surveyor of those shores. A schooner, the *Grenville*, was placed under his command, and in April he sailed for his station. Every autumn he returned to England, and every spring he went out again. This is proved by the dates of his children's births. The work lasted till the year 1767. During these four years he executed a great amount of surveying, and drew charts which are still in use. He also explored a part of that great island of Newfoundland, the interior of which is still almost as little known as in the days when Cook discovered its chain of lakes and followed up the streams. In 1766 he contributed a paper to the Royal Society of London, entitled "An Observation of an Eclipse of the Sun at the Island of Newfoundland,

5th August 1766, with the Longitude of the Place of Observation deduced from it." There were not many officers in the Royal Navy of that time who were capable of taking such an observation, or of making any deductions from it.

In the autumn of 1767 he returned home, his work in America completed, and thus the second chapter of his life closed. He was now thirty-nine years of age; he had been at sea for twenty five years. But the best part of his life was before him; all its honour, its highest interest, its best excitement, its greatest rewards. What followed were years of endurance and hardship; he was prepared for them by his long service on the cold and stormy waters of the German Ocean, by the rough and simple fare on which he had subsisted from childhood, by his long companionship with rough and illiterate sailors, whose wants, whose virtues, and whose vices he knew better than any other officer of his time.

One knows not what may have been his ambition; probably to continue in survey work and cartography; one hardly supposes that, after such an office as Cook had held in Newfoundland, he would greatly desire to sail as master even on a first-rater. He could hardly have looked for such work as fell into his hands. Many men, it is said, fail because they never get a chance of showing the world what they can do. This may be true of one or two professions, the bar, for instance, or medicine, but it is not true of any other calling. Least of all is it the case in the services, where a man must be discovered if he be a good man. There is, however, a better way of putting it. Many a man might rise to the highest distinction, as well as those who do, had they the chance. As it is, their chances lead them only to the lower heights. Thus there may have been other men in the service as well qualified as James Cook to command on a voyage of *Discovery*. I doubt it, but there may have been. The man was ready, the chance came to him, and he proved himself equal to his fortune.

CHAPTER IV

THE GREAT UNKNOWN OCEAN

ON the 25th day of September, in the year 1513, Balboa first caught sight of the great Pacific Ocean.

For two hundred years and more the Spaniards regarded the Pacific as their own possession; the sea seemed closed to the world, except by one difficult and dangerous portal. This entrance itself was defended not only by its difficulties and dangers, but by a strange superstition. Everybody, it was observed, who had to do with the first passage by Magellan came to a bad end. The captain was murdered in a brawl by the natives of the Philippines; Ruy Falero, one of his company, died raving mad; the sailor De Lepe, who first sighted the straits from the mast-head, was taken prisoner by the Algerians, became renegade, and embraced the faith of the False Prophet, by which, of course, he lost his everlasting soul. Nay, Balboa himself was beheaded. And when ships afterwards began to attempt the straits, they were constantly driven back by winds and storms, which seemed to have been engaged in the service of the Castilian king.

The first, however, to sail upon these waters was Ponce de Leon, two years after their *Discovery*. He caused two or three small boats to be carried across the isthmus, and sailed along the coast about Panama. In the year 1517 he founded the city of Panama, four miles from its present site. He also attempted to build ships on the Pacific coast, but was forced to desist, because the timber he used became instantly penetrated and devoured by worms.

Let us follow briefly in this chapter the history of *Discovery* in the Pacific Ocean from the first launch of Ponce de Leon's boats to the time when Cook sailed upon his first voyage. You may take a great sheet of paper and lay down on its eastern side a short line of the coast round Panama; on the western side some imperfect fragments of the great islands of Borneo, Sumatra, and Java. The whole of the sheet, save for these fragments, must be painted black, it is absolutely unknown. As one navigator after another traverses the ocean, a new line of light runs out wherever he leaves the beaten track. Each voyage outside that beaten track leaves a belt of light no more than twenty miles in breadth. You will see that even after two hundred and fifty years the blackness of great portions is wholly unrelieved by any such broad line of light. You will understand by such a method what kind of task lay before the men who set forth upon a voyage of *Discovery* upon those unknown waters.

It was only six years after the *Discovery* by Balboa, namely in the year 1519, that Magellan found and passed through the straits which bear his name; when he emerged into the Pacific his idea was to sail across to the Moluccas; he therefore held a N.W. course, one which, unfortunately for him, caused him to pass by all the great archipelagos and the coast of Australia. He found certain small islands, but their names and positions cannot with any certainty be laid down. His ship reached the Moluccas in safety, but without her captain, who was lying buried in the Philippines.

In the year 1525 a very important expedition was sent out to the Pacific by the King of Spain. It was commanded by Don Garcia Jofre de Loyasa, and consisted of seven ships and four hundred and fifty men. He achieved the passage of the straits in safety, coasted Chile and Peru, and having reached the latitude of 13° N. he steered a westward course along that parallel and arrived at the Ladrones. His course was afterwards blindly followed by the Spaniards, which was the cause why, while they held almost undisturbed possession of those seas, they made no progress in its exploration. It was Loyasa who discovered the north coast of Papua. Meantime, in the far east, the extension of trade was causing the *Discovery* of new lands. Sanvedra, sailing from Gilolo, followed the coast of Papua for a good distance, and discovered in lat. 5° N. the islands which he called Los Pintados and Los Buenos Jardines. In 1542 Japan was first visited.

In the same year Villalobos crossed the Pacific on the same parallel as Loyasa. After this very little was done for some years. Many attempts proved failures: some through the difficulties of the straits, some through bad weather, some through the death of the captain. The islands of Juan Fernandez and Masafuera were discovered in 1563; those of the Galapagos in 1550.

A chart of the Pacific in the middle of the sixteenth century, about fifty or sixty years after its *Discovery*, shows the western coast of South America laid down tolerably well, except that of Southern Chile; the coast of North America has been followed as far north as California, which in some maps appears as an island, and in others as a peninsula. On the eastern side of the chart one observes a part of China, a part of Japan, the Philippines, Celebes, Timor, and the Ladrones. There are one or two small islands laid down with no certainty of latitude or longitude, and the north coast of Papua is indicated. Nothing whatever is as yet known of Australia and New Zealand. There is, however, an imaginary southern continent laid down with great boldness. The existence of Terra Australis Incognita had in fact already begun to haunt men's minds. It was said that Juan Fernandez had actually landed on this continent and found there a white people, civilised, well formed, well clothed. It was within a month's sail of Chile. But no one else ever found this continent.

It was in the year 1573 that Drake climbed the hill and the tree upon its summit from which could be seen both the Atlantic and the Pacific Oceans. "Almighty God!" he exclaimed, "of Thy goodness give me life and leave to sail once in an English ship upon that sea." Now there was with the party that day an Englishman named John Oxenham, spelt Oxnam. This man, a fellow full of *Resolution*, conceived a brilliant project. He would get together a party, cross the isthmus with them, capture first a small ship and then a big ship, and rove the seas, plundering the Spaniards and sailing whithersoever they listed. He partly carried this project into execution. That is to say, he got together his company, crossed the isthmus, and falling upon a small craft in the Bay of Panama took possession of it. No more curious story belongs to this time of adventure. But the attempt ended badly, because the party were not strong enough to take a bigger ship and had to run ashore, where they were all captured and hanged. Thus the Pacific destroyed the first Englishman as well as the first Spaniard who attempted it. The toll of blood thus exacted, the ocean lay open to Drake. It is remarkable that he coasted North America to lat. 48° N. in the hope of finding a passage to the Atlantic. Two hundred years later Cook went out upon exactly the same errand.

The way being now known, the distance, and the comparative safety of the passage, voyages across the Pacific from New Spain to the Philippines and back again now began to be not infrequent. Many accounts remain of such voyages; from America westward the ships always kept in the same parallel, that of 13° N., as nearly as possible. There was a fair wind and an open sea. The voyage generally took eighty days. From the Philippines to New Spain the same course could not be always kept, but there was little deviation.

The English, meanwhile, were by no means unmindful of this ocean, into which Drake had led the way. Two or three unsuccessful attempts were made, that in the year 1582 by Edward Fenton and Luke Ward to get through the straits; that in 1587 by Withrington and Lister.

But in 1586 Cavendish sailed with his squadron of three ships, the *Desire* of one hundred and twenty tons, the *Content* of sixty, and the *Hugh Gallant* of forty, with crews numbering one hundred and twenty-three in all, and carrying two years' provisions. He sailed along the coast as far north as California, thence steered on a south-westerly course for the Ladrones. On the way, as all the world knows, he fell in with the great plate galleon and captured her. Never was such a splendid prize as that of this great ship. She had 122,000 pesos of gold on board, besides an immense quantity of satins, silk, musk, and all kinds of precious things. Naturally this good fortune stimulated imitators. Cavendish himself made a second attempt, but the great galleon was not to be taken by every one. One after the other half a dozen attempts were made, and all failed. In 1594 Sir Richard Hawkins, for instance, had the bad luck to be taken prisoner, he and his ship the *Dainty*. Such a misfortune daunted even the English courage for a while. In the course of these voyages, however, the Falkland Islands were discovered by Captain John Davis, who had already made three attempts to find the North-West passage, and whose name survives in our maps in Davis' Straits.

Meantime the Spaniards continued their voyages of *Discovery*, but in a languid way, having indeed already more upon their hands than they could well manage. Mendana, in 1595, departing from the usual track, sailed across the ocean, following as closely as possible lat. 14° S. He was rewarded by the *Discovery* of the Marquesas, New Hebrides, and Santa Cruz groups, and in 1600 a Spanish expedition was sent to sail along the west coast of North America. Towards the end of this century the Dutch appeared in these seas. In 1595 the "Five Ship" expedition from Rotterdam set sail; they followed the usual line, but steered northwards and touched at Japan. In 1598 Oliver van Noort made the now familiar voyage in lat. 13° N.

During the seventeenth century the troubles and civil wars at home kept the English quiet. It is the century of the Dutch. The Spaniards, however, in the course of a voyage in search of the southern continent discovered, it was in 1606, the coast of Terra Australis.

As for the Dutch, they sent out Joris Spilbergen in 1615, who sailed up the coast and defeated the Spanish fleet. They sent out Le Maire and Schouten, who discovered the Strait of Le Maire, to the great uneasiness of the Spaniards; they also found the Admiralty Islands and New Ireland. In 1626 the great Nassau fleet sailed round the world, but seems to have done little. In 1639 the Dutch sent out an expedition to examine the east coast of Great Tartary and to discover the Gold and Silver Islands. But of course the greatest Dutch navigator was Tasman, whose famous voyage was begun from Batavia in the year 1642. It was not until 1667 that the French sailed upon the Pacific.

In 1670 Captain Narborough made his chart of the Straits of Magellan. This was the only important British voyage of *Discovery* belonging to the century. To the end of this century belongs the period of the Buccaneers, which has been already treated at length in this series by Mr. Clark Russell in his Life of Dampier. The adventures of the *Cygnet*, the *Roebuck*, the *Cinque Ports*, the *Duke*, and the *Duchess*, the names of Morgan, Sawkins, Dampier, Edward Cooke, Woodes Rogers, Clapperton, and Shelvocke, belong to the Rovers; those of Commodore Anson, Byron, Wallis, and Carteret to the time when the Spaniards could no longer pretend, even on the authority of the Pope, to regard the Pacific as their private lake. No nation in the world has ever had such splendid opportunities as Spain. One reads at school how Athens, when its population grew too large, could ship off a whole colony to some island not far removed, one envies the simplicity of emigration in those days. But a far greater ocean than the Mediterranean was given to the Spaniards. From the year 1513, when the Pacific was discovered, down to the middle of the eighteenth century, that is to say, for two hundred and fifty years, the Spaniard lived secure, fearing no danger, from generation to generation, in the warm air that he loved, with a subject race to work for him, in luxury, at ease, without anxiety, and wealthy beyond any dream possible to the proud and poor hidalgo of the mother country. It was an ideal life. And it lasted for eight long generations. During this time there was, doubtless, a continual stream from the old world of those who wished to share in these good things. Those who came first got the best; but there was enough and to spare had the Spaniard continued to possess the spirit of enterprise. But he did not; he gave no welcome to fresh blood, he lost the old spirit of adventure; he even lost his old courage; he became greedy, jealous, and lazy. Had such a chance come to Great Britain, every island in the Pacific would have been explored long before the eighteenth century; and if there had not been planted upon every island a little colony of ruling Britons under their native flag, it would have been because there were not enough Britons to go round.

I say that the Spaniards were practically undisturbed. What did the successful raids of Drake, Cavendish, and the rest amount to in all? Once or twice the English devils took the great galleon. But only once or twice in all these years. Now and again, a town was assaulted and taken by these pirates. But how many towns were taken? How often were towns taken? There was fighting at Panama, at Guayaquil, at Acapulco, at Payta, but where else? The Spanish Americans feared little danger; they ran few risks; from generation to generation they grew richer and lazier; the old courage of the Spaniard had entirely left him by the third generation; he could no longer fight; life had become too easy for him. But he remained in possession because there were none to turn him out.

All this was changed by the middle of the eighteenth century. It seemed as if the great southern continent was actually going to be discovered at last, and that it would not belong to Spain; an immense and apparently wealthy country called Papua was now known to exist; Japan and China had to be reckoned with; the Dutch had possession of Java and were pushing eastwards; English ships were exploring the ocean, once the Spaniard's own ocean, in all directions; the French themselves, last in the field, had appeared; and it was evident to all that Spain could no longer even pretend to keep out the other nations. And, besides, the English brain was fired with the thought of the Pacific, as in Queen Elizabeth's time it had been fired with the thought of the West Indies. Reports came home of lovely islands; the English, though as yet they knew nothing of Hawaii or Tahiti, had heard of Juan Fernandez and Masafuera; they had read the Voyages of Woodes Rogers, of Clapperton and Shelvocke; with Anson they had visited the lovely Tinian, with its strange avenues of pillars; they knew of the Galapagos, the sea-lions of California, the Spice Islands and the Ladrones, the Tierra del Fuego and its miserable people.

The long smouldering theory of the southern continent revived again. Scientific men proved beyond a doubt that the right balance of the globe required a southern continent; otherwise it would of course tip over. Geographers pointed out how Quiros, Juan Fernandez, and Tasman had all touched at various points of that continent. Men of imagination spoke of treasures of all kinds which would be found there, and would belong to the nation which should discover and annex this land; they laid it down on the maps and reckoned up the various kinds of climate which would be enjoyed in a country stretching from the Southern Pole through forty degrees of latitude. The most extravagant ideas were formed of what might be found; fictitious travels fed the imagination of the people; men confidently looked forward to acquiring a prolonged rule over other golden lands, such as had been for nearly three hundred years the making and the unmaking of Spain. In every age there is always a grasping after what seems to promise the sovereignty of the world. In every age there is a Carthage to be destroyed; and in every age there are half a dozen countries each of which is eager and anxious to enact the part of Rome.

Such is, in brief outline, the story, many times told but always new, of the principal voyages of *Discovery* on the great Pacific Ocean. It would be tedious and beyond these limits to attempt further details or to follow the tracks of these hardy sailors. To those who love a tale of peril and of courage, there is no better reading than that of the old voyagers from Columbus, the first of modern navigators, down to Captain Cook, the last.

We have seen the chart of the Pacific at the end of the sixteenth century. Let us look at it in the eighteenth before Cook began to sail upon it. The chart of 1750 shows a very considerable advance upon that of 1570. In the map attached to Gordon's *Geography* of 1740 there are certain instructive and suggestive things. For instance, New Guinea and New Holland are united. Only the west coast of New Holland is given; there is a small corner or angle of land which represents the whole of New Zealand. California is an island; the Ladrones are named and lie between lat. 10° N. and 20° S. There are also certain scattered groups of islands nameless, and apparently set down at random. The map is exactly similar to that illustrating Shelvocke's voyage (1726), save that in Shelvocke's map the islands are named.

Turning to the letterpress, Gordon says, under the heading of "Terra Magellanica": "Many things equally foolish as ridiculous are related of this country and its inhabitants, with which I shall neither trouble myself or the reader." And in Section XIII, "Concerning Terra Australis," he says:

By Terra Antarctica we understand all those unknown or slenderly discovered countries towards the southern Parts of the Globe; the chief of which do bear the names of New Guinea, New Zealand, New Holland, and (which may comprehend them and all the rest) *Terra Australis Incognita.* Which southern countries, though they belong not to the continent of America, yet we choose to mention them in this place, since the southmost part of the continent of S. America doth extend itself farther towards the S. than any Part or Headland of the old Continent... Leaving them therefore to the *Discovery* of future ages, we pass on.

NOTE TO CHAPTER IV

THE following is a complete list of voyages round the world from Magellan to Anson.

	Sailed from	Sailed.	Returned.
Ferdinand Magellan	Seville	Aug. 10, 1519	Sept. 8, 1522
Sir Francis Drake	Plymouth	Dec. 20, 1577	Sept. 16, 1580
Sir Thomas Cavendish	Do.	July 25, 1586	Sept. 9, 1588
Oliver van Noord	Goeree	Sept. 13, 1598	Aug. 26, 1601
George Spilbergen	Texel	Aug. 8, 1614	July 1, 1617
The Nassau Fleet& Le Maire	Schouten	June 24, 1615	Do.
Cooke, Cowley, and Dampier	Virginia	Aug. 23, 1683	Jan. 21, 1686
William Dampier	Do.	Do.	Oct. 12, 1686
Dampier and Funnel	The Downs	Aug. 9, 1703	Sept. 16, 1706
Woodes Rogers and Courtney	Bristol	June 15, 1708	Aug. 1, 1711
John Clapperton	Plymouth	Feb. 15, 1719	June 1722
George Shelvocke	Do.	Do.	Aug. 1, 1722
Roggewein	Texel	July 17, 1721	July 11, 1723
Commodore Anson	St. Helens	Sept. 18, 1740	June 15, 1744

CHAPTER V

COOK'S THREE PREDECESSORS

So greatly has the fame of Cook eclipsed that of his predecessors, that we are inclined to forget that his century produced other great navigators besides himself. Not to speak of foreign expeditions, there were the voyages of Anson, Byron, Wallis, and Carteret, which must, in justice to Cook himself, be touched upon before his own voyages are considered. Commodore Anson's course presents no features of great interest. Like most of the early navigators, he steered northward after passing through the Straits of Magellan, touched at Juan Fernandez, coasted South America, stood in at Panama, went out to sea again, appeared off Acapulco, and then sailed in the parallel of 13° N. to the Ladrones. He added little to the geography of the world.

Commodore Byron's voyage (1764-1766) was almost as barren of results, although like Magellan he seemed to avoid discovering the archipelagos between which he passed by a kind of miracle. He had with him the *Dolphin*, a man-of-war of the sixth rate, carrying thirty-six guns, with a complement of three lieutenants, thirty-seven petty officers, and one hundred and fifty men, and the *Tamar* sloop, sixteen guns, under Captain Mowat, with three lieutenants, twenty-seven petty officers, and ninety men. His general instructions were to sail in the southern seas and to make such discoveries and observations as he should find possible. These instructions were not communicated to the men until they were well out at sea. Double pay was promised, with other advantages. He sailed to Port Desire, north of the Straits, sighting the Falkland Islands on the way. He then sailed into the Straits as far as Port Famine, when he was forced to put back again. He visited the Falklands, they had formerly been known as Hawkins's Maiden Land or Pepys' Land, and then made another attempt to get through the Straits. They entered this terrible strait on Sunday, February 17th, and came out of it on Tuesday, April 9th, that is to say, the passage of the Straits took them fifty-one days, which must not be considered a very long time, considering the time spent by some ships in the passage. Captain Wallis afterwards spent four months getting through. De Bougainville took one day longer than Byron. The weather during the whole time that Byron was in the Straits he describes as "dreadful beyond all description."

On April 26th the ships were off Masafuera. After leaving this island Byron sailed north into lat. 26° S., when, like Magellan, he took a W.N.W. course, and ran half-way across the ocean without sighting any land. He then arrived at the northern end of the Society Islands, discovering certain of the smaller outlying islands, but missing Tahiti and the more important places. He then sailed N.W. for the Ladrones, discovering one or two insignificant islands on the way.

It is an interesting voyage, but one feels that the gallant commodore was not anxious to linger, and, indeed, his crew were suffering too much from scurvy to allow further delay. Captain Cook, in his place, would have put in at some island where he could have relieved and refreshed his men, and would then have turned back. But it is not every commander who can discover islands; Byron had not *la main heureuse*. Nor is it every commander who loves the perils of an unknown sea. Byron on his return was made Governor of Newfoundland, and afterwards commanded a fleet to oppose the Comte d'Estaign in 1777. He died in 1786.

The *Dolphin*, being refitted, was sent out again in the year of her return, under command of Captain Samuel Wallis, who had with him the *Swallow* sloop, Captain Carteret, and the *Prince Frederick* store-ship. Great attention was paid on this voyage to the shipment of medicines, portable soup, and other things for the prevention of scurvy. The ships sailed on August 22nd, 1766; they entered the Straits on December 17th, 1766, and did not get out of it until April 11th, 1767. They actually spent four months trying to work through this abominable passage, which is, if one understands Wallis aright, about eight hundred and eighty miles in length. Wallis made, however, a careful chart of the whole Straits, and wrote a description of the navigation for use by those who should come after him.

On leaving the Straits the *Dolphin*, sailing much faster than the *Swallow*, lost sight of her. "I would have shortened sail for the *Swallow*" says Captain Wallis, " but it was not in my power, for as a current set us strongly down upon the Isles of Direction, and the wind came to the west, it became absolutely necessary for me to carry sail, so that I might clear them. Soon after we lost sight of the *Swallow*, and never saw her again." To the people on the latter vessel it looked as if Captain Wallis had crowded sail with the deliberate intention of deserting them.

Wallis made no land for seven weeks, when they discovered a small island or two. About this time the diet of salt beef and pork began to produce their usual result in the appearance of scurvy. The men began to fall down very fast. Vinegar and mustard were served out, as antiscorbutics, as much as the men chose to take; wine was given instead of spirits, also sweet wort and saloop: portable soup was also boiled with their peas and oatmeal; the berths were kept clean, the hammocks were frequently washed, the water was rendered wholesome by ventilation, and every part between decks frequently washed with vinegar. Yet the scurvy continued to spread. Nor was it until they reached a land where fruit and green food could be procured that the men recovered. These preventive measures are necessary to notice in view of their helplessness and the sanitary improvements introduced by Cook on his second voyage.

Early in June Wallis entered the archipelago of the Society Islands on the south-east side, discovering island after island, until they reached Tahiti, which Wallis named King George the Third's Island. It was fortunate for Cook that his predecessor left behind him a kindly memory among the natives, though their friendship began with a fight. Wallis's account of the place and the people occupies a great part of his narrative. It is not so full and complete as the accounts afterwards given by Cook, by George Forster, Anderson, and King, but it is highly curious and interesting. No island of the Pacific has been more thoroughly described as it appeared on its first *Discovery* than Tahiti. Of that pristine simplicity of manners how much now remains? From the Society Islands Wallis steered W., and afterwards N.W., for Tinian and the Ladrones, another example of the way in which sailors, one after the other, used to make for the known points. Had he continued a westerly course, he would have struck the coast of New Holland; had he steered S.W., he would have anticipated Cook and discovered New Zealand. Satisfied, however, with the glory of finding King George the Third's Island, he made for the Ladrones. On the way he found several small islands.

Here follows a very curious and tragic little story.

On arriving at Java he found H.M.S. *Falmouth* lying in the mud in a rotten condition; her ports were broken, her stern post decayed, and there was no place in the ship where a man could be sheltered from the weather. The few people who belonged to her had been left in charge. It is not stated how long, or in what circumstances they had been left there, or what had become of the ship's officers. The story is an illustration of the delights which awaited a sailor at that time. These people were the petty officers, and, one supposes, some of the crew. The decaying ship lay rotting in the stinking tropical mud while the men in charge waited for orders from England. None came. The Dutch refused to let them sleep on shore. When they were sick no one would visit them on board. They were afraid that the Malays would come and murder them, and set their ship on fire. The stores which they were left to guard had all been destroyed, their powder had been thrown into the water by the Dutch. The masts, yards, and cables were all dropping to pieces, and even the ironwork was so rusty that it was no longer worth anything. Ten years' pay was due to them. They had actually been in this horrible place for ten years. They were growing old in this misery. They expected that the next monsoon would break up the rotten old ship and drown them. Could there be a more miserable condition? The gunner was dead, the boatswain had gone mad, the carpenter was dying, and the cook was a wounded cripple. Wallis refused to relieve them. They were left in charge, he said, and they must wait for orders from home. So he sailed away. Nothing more is recorded of these poor fellows; but the year after, Carteret, who put in at Batavia for repairs, mentions the *Falmouth* as a ship that had been condemned. One hopes that somehow the survivors had been taken home, and were already in the enjoyment of their ten years' pay. But one fears that their last home was in the warm mud of that fatal creek.

The *Dolphin* anchored in the Downs six hundred and thirty-seven days after her departure from Plymouth Sound. This was a very quick voyage, but, as has been evident from the course taken, it was straight across the ocean. The voyage of the little *Swallow*, under Carteret, who had already sailed round the world with Byron, was by far the most interesting of any before those of Cook. It was also the most perilous. The vessel selected for this long and dangerous service was a sloop, thirty years old. She was thinly sheathed, and provided with nothing more than the barest necessaries. The captain, in considering the scanty equipment of the vessel, was persuaded that the *Swallow* was not intended to sail farther than the Falkland Isles. In this he was undeceived.

The two ships kept in company, as already stated, through the Straits, when the *Dolphin* sailed away, leaving her consort alone, and without appointing any rendezvous. None of the stores necessary to obtain refreshments from the natives, cloth, linen, beads, scissors, etc., were on board the *Swallow*, which was also unprovided even with a forge or any iron. And at the outset the ship was so foul that even with all sails set she could not keep up with the Dolphin, though the latter was sailing under topsails alone. After a month of storm and rain with heavy seas the little vessel arrived at Masafuera.

And now began in earnest a voyage, with which none other can be compared, for the *Resolution* of the captain and the perils and discomforts of the ship's company. With a small vessel, imperfectly found, without even the means of repairing a broken cable, the commander would have been perfectly justified either in steering the shortest course across the Pacific or in returning home through the

Straits. Carteret, with the true spirit of a navigator, did neither. He cruised about in search of doubtful places. He looked for certain islands laid down in Green's chart of 1753, and also in Robertson's *Elements of Navigation*, and proved at least that their position was wrongly laid down, even if the islands had any existence. In these days of imperfect observation the true longitudes were generally arrived at after repeated visits and many observations. He also proved that the so-called Davis's Land, supposed to be a part of the great southern continent, did not exist, at least in the place assigned to it. He discovered Pitcairn's Island, but was unable to effect a landing. He then, like Byron and Wallis, sailed into the archipelago of the Society Islands, but lighted on the southern group. The ship beginning to grow crazy, and the crew being sick with scurvy, Carteret was compelled to abandon his wish to steer S.E. Had he been able to do so, he might have anticipated many of Cook's discoveries. He therefore followed a N.W. course. But not, as "Wallis and Byron before him, making for the Ladrones, and so by the north of the Philippines to Batavia. Carteret kept as long as possible south of the equator. He discovered the Queen Charlotte Islands, he discovered and sailed through New Britain and New Ireland, he discovered the Admiralty Islands, Joseph Freewill's Island, examined the coast of Mindanao, sailed round Celebes, and so arrived at Batavia. Had he been able to land, procure refreshments, and repair his vessel, he would have steered S.E. after leaving Queen Charlotte Islands.

Hitherto (he says), though I had long been ill of an inflammatory and bilious disorder, I had been able to keep the deck; but this evening the symptoms became so much more threatening that I could keep up no longer, and I was for some time afterwards confined to my bed. The master was dying of the wounds he received in his quarrel with the Indians, the lieutenant also was very ill, the gunner and thirty of my men incapable of duty, among whom were some of the most vigorous and healthy, that had been wounded with the master, and three of them mortally ; and there was no hope of obtaining such refreshments as we most needed in the place. These were discouraging circumstances, and not only put an end to my hopes of prosecuting the voyage farther to southward, but greatly dispirited the people; except myself, the master, and the lieutenant, there was nobody on board capable of navigating a ship home. The master was known to be a dying man, and the recovery of myself and the lieutenant was very doubtful. I would, however, have made a further effort to obtain refreshments here if I had been furnished with any toys, iron tools, or cutlery ware, which might have enabled me to recover the goodwill of the natives, and establish a traffic with them for such necessaries as they would have furnished us with. But I had no such articles, and but very few others fit for an Indian trade; and not being in a condition to risk the loss of any more of the few men who were capable of doing duty, I weighed anchor at daybreak on Monday the 12th, and stood along the shore for that part of the island to which I had sent the cutter.

When the ship at last arrived at Macassar every man on board was ill with scurvy, and the Dutch, in their usual spirit, refused any assistance.

On March 20th, 1769, nearly a year after Captain Wallis's return, the *Swallow* anchored at Spithead. The explanations of the former officer, when the two gallant captains met, are not on record.

I have thought it just both to Cook and to the memory of these three, his immediate predecessors, to give a somewhat more detailed account of their voyages. It will be observed that the zeal with which Carteret carried out his instructions differed essentially from that which the other two brought to their enterprise. Byron and Wallis had large and well-found ships. Yet they hastened to get out of the Pacific as quickly as possible, and by that part of it already known. Carteret had a small and ill-found old and crazy craft. De Bougainville, who passed the *Swallow* homeward bound, reports that "Carteret's ship was very small, went very ill, and when we took leave of him, remained as it were at anchor. How much he must have suffered in so bad a vessel may well be conceived." He had a sick crew and could get no refreshments. Yet he lingered as long as he could in the .ocean, and but for impossibility would have explored the southeast Pacific, then wholly unknown. Perhaps the known zeal of the younger man caused Wallis to sail out of sight as quickly as possible after passing through the Straits.

The chart of the Pacific, therefore, had been enriched, as the result of these three voyages, first by the group of the Society Islands, of which Byron discovered the northern isles, Wallis Tahiti, and Carteret those to the south. Byron and Wallis did little more. Carteret discovered the Queen Charlotte Islands, Pitcairn's Island, separated New Britain from New Ireland, and found other small islands.

CHAPTER VI

COOK'S FIRST VOYAGE

WE have now cleared the way for a right understanding of Cook's voyages and their results. We have seen the Pacific Ocean at first a great black sheet, streaked with thin belts of light as one voyager after the other ventured across. On the north of the equator, along the parallel of 13° N., there is a broad belt, this is the highway between Panama and Manila. In spite of many voyages there is still little light upon the central and south Pacific. By far the greater part of the ocean is covered with thick darkness.

In considering these expeditions one is faced by certain difficulties which do not apply to the earlier voyages. It is that they belong almost to our own time, that their history has been narrated over and over again. Every boy has read Cook's Voyages; not only every library, but almost every house with a row of bookshelves contains some account of them; there are cheap and popular editions, there are illustrated editions; they have been abridged, condensed, and castigated for the use of the young; they have served for lectures, illustrated by the magic lantern; they are known, in scraps, by everybody. That is to say, though few of us would sit down to pass an examination on the subject, we all know in general terms that Cook surveyed the coasts of New Zealand and New Holland, penetrated the southern ocean, traversed the Pacific in every direction, and was finally murdered at the island which some of us still, faithful to tradition, call Owhyhee. Again, all the anecdotes, the interesting facts, the dramatic bits, have long since been picked out, over and over again, so that they cannot be reproduced with the slightest show of freshness. Cook is not yet so old that, like Dampier and Shelvocke, only historical geographers and the people who read everything know him; nor is he still so young that his achievements may bear another description by a new hand.

He is, again, not yet so old but that men are still living who have conversed with survivors of the crews of Wallis, Carteret, and Cook. A man of twenty-five on board the *Endeavour* in 1768 would be no more than seventy-seven in 1820; a man of twenty-five on board the *Resolution* in 1779 might live to reach eighty-six in 1840. There are among us some who can still remember the year 1820, and many who can remember the year 1840. It is, indeed, wonderful how far back one can reach in this way. It is not very long since some of Nelson's old tars still lingered, and lightened the tedium of time spent in sitting on a bench in the Common Hard above the Logs, by telling over again the story of the battles they had fought and the victories they had won. Nay, there might have been among them, perchance, as late as 1850, some more aged man, one who had witnessed from the boats of the *Resolution* the murder on the beach of Owhyhee; there may have been a solitary survivor or two of that tragedy lingering on in their nineties. And as to grandsons of those hardy mariners, there are many still living, though, unfortunately, none of the great captain himself.

Considering this difficulty, therefore, it will be prudent not to follow each of these voyages in detail, seeing that to do so would be to present a tale ten times told already, but to draw up a skeleton route or course of each in turn, with such illustrations as may be gathered, not so much from the official journals and descriptions which have been used over and over again, but from such other contemporary documents as are not generally known or are not easily accessible, and especially such illustrations as serve to show the personal character of the commander himself and the kind of company which manned his ships. As for the places which he visited, and the people whom he brought to light, are they not described already in the books? We are not here considering the manners and customs of the Polynesians; their origin, language, religion, folklore, and relationships do not concern us.

The Royal Society, discovering that there would happen a transit of Venus in the year 1769, and that this interesting astronomical event would be best observed from some place in the Pacific Ocean, drew up a memorial to the king, praying that an expedition might be sent out with that object. They proposed, as the most convenient station of any then known, the islands of Rotterdam, Amsterdam, or the Marquesas. The memorial was favourably received, and the king consented to grant a ship properly provisioned and equipped to carry out any scientific observer who should be appointed by the Society. Mr. Alexander Dalrymple, a well-known student and writer on geography and Fellow of the Society, was at first proposed as the commander of the scientific expedition. He consented to go, thinking that he should not only lead the scientific party but would also command the ship, as had been done on a previous occasion, when Dr. Halley, for scientific purposes, was put in command of a ship, with brevet rank as captain. But the Admiralty, also bearing in mind the example of Dr. Halley, and its results in mutiny and disorders, refused absolutely to put another landsman, with no knowledge whatever of discipline, in command of a ship. On so long a voyage the results would certainly be far worse than on that occasion. Sir Edward Hawke, then at the head of the Admiralty, plainly declared that he would cut off his right hand rather than sign a commission for a person who was not a sailor. Then Mr. Dalrymple first refused to go at all, and then wanted to go; and finally, when it was too late, seems to have sulked, and ever afterwards complained that he had been badly treated by the Admiralty. They then cast about for an officer who could not only command the ship but also conduct the scientific purpose of the expedition. No other man could be found than James Cook, master in the Royal Navy. Everything happened fortunately and opportunely for him; he had just returned from the important post of surveyor of Newfoundland and Labrador; he was therefore available, and on the spot. He had brought himself into great notice by his admirable charts, and he was well recommended by every officer under whom he had served. It is indeed most probable that no other officer in the navy possessed so much scientific knowledge as Cook. To have mastered the whole art of navigation, with the methods and tactics of naval warfare in all its branches, was then considered an education sufficient for the best and most ambitious officer. Yet one doubts whether Cook would have received the appointment had either Wallis or Carteret returned in time. Their experience of the Pacific would have outweighed Cook's proved zeal, intelligence, and scientific attainments. However, Cook was recommended by Mr. Stephens, Secretary to the Admiralty, and no other officer seems to have been considered at all. Certainly the command of an expedition, not warlike, from which no glory of the usual kind could be obtained, certain to be long and tedious, and equally certain to be full of dangers and discomforts, was not a post for which backstairs influence would be employed, or favouritism brought into request.

Cook accepted the offer eagerly and instantly. It was indeed an enormous step upwards; he was taken out of the master's line, from which there was seldom any promotion possible, and placed into the higher branch; he received the rank of lieutenant.

In his introduction to the narrative of the second voyage, Cook explains what kind of ship is best for the successful conduct of such enterprises. He says:

The success.... will more chiefly depend on the kind, the size, and the properties of the ships chosen for the service ... as the greatest danger to be apprehended and provided against on a voyage of *Discovery*, especially to the most distant parts of the globe, is that of the ship's being liable to be run aground on an unknown desert, or perhaps savage coast. So no consideration should be set in competition with that of her being of a construction of the safest kind, in which the officers may, with the least hazard, venture upon a strange coast. A ship of this kind must not be of a great draught of water, yet of a sufficient burden and capacity to carry a proper quantity of provisions and necessaries for her complement of men, and for the term requisite to perform the voyage.

She must also be of a construction that will bear to take the ground, and of a size which, in case of necessity, may be safely and conveniently laid on shore to repair any accidental damage or defect. These properties are not to be found in ships of war of forty guns, nor in frigates, nor in East India Company's ships, nor in large three-decked West India ships, nor indeed in any other but North-country-built ships, as such as are built for the coal trade, which are peculiarly adapted for this purpose.

After this expression of opinion, written, it is true, after his experience on the first voyage, it is not surprising to learn that his first ship, the *Endeavour*, was in fact a collier, built by his old friends of Whitby, a stout, strong ship, designed for safety in all weathers rather than for speed. Her like still sails between the northern ports and London. She herself, until a few years ago, carried on at a very advanced age the trade for which she was originally constructed. She was of three hundred and seventy tons.

The scientific party consisted of Mr. Charles Green, one of the assistants to the Astronomer-Royal; Joseph Banks (afterwards Sir Joseph), a man of large private means, and already of considerable scientific reputation; Dr. Solander, one of the assistants of the British Museum. Banks brought with him a naturalist, Mr. Sydney Parkinson a draughtsman, and others as assistants. The *Endeavour's* complement consisted of eighty-five men in all, including the captain, two lieutenants, three midshipmen, a master, surgeon, boatswain, carpenter, and the other petty officers, with forty-one able seamen, twelve marines, and nine servants. She took on board ten carriage and twelve swivel guns, and was provisioned for eighteen months.

Before the *Endeavour* was fitted out Captain Wallis returned, bringing the news of the discovery of Otaheite (George Forster, of the second voyage, spells it O-Taheiti, which is nearer to its new name of Tahiti). And as the place seemed more convenient than the Marquesas for astronomical observation, it was determined that the transit should be observed from Otaheite.

The *Endeavour* was fitted in the basin of Deptford dockyard July 30th, 1768. She sailed from Deptford, and on August 26th, the wind being fair, she put to sea from Plymouth. The superstitious may remark that this most successful voyage of *Discovery* was commenced on a Friday.

The only account of the voyage is that published officially. Most unfortunately it is not the work of Cook himself, or of Banks, whose journals were extremely voluminous; it is a clumsy compilation by Dr. Hawkesworth, into whose hands were placed all the journals, logs, and other papers connected with the voyages of Byron, Wallis, Carteret, and Cook, the first voyage only of the last named. It was fondly thought that this writer, then a well-known *litterateur*, would be able to present the separate journals in a narrative possessing the graces of literary style. This the doctor undertook to do, with the understanding that he was at liberty to decorate the naked narrative with remarks or sentiments of his own proper to the occasion. As the narrative is written in the first person, as if by the respective officers whose names stand at the head of each history, the result is truly wonderful. It must be owned that the author of this literary job was careful to preserve every incident recorded in the journals, yet their mode of presentment robbed the journals entirely of the personal element which is the chief charm in all books of travel. Wallis and Carteret have disappeared altogether. Cook himself is invisible under the classic garments with which he is arrayed. The sentiments, it is true, are beautiful; there is a display of learning which makes the memory of the Free Love of Whitby seem like a bad dream. Cook must surely have been wandering all these years on the banks of Granta. For instance, how judicious is the rendering of such a simple incident as that described in the following passage: "The scene might possibly have become more curious and interesting if it had not suddenly been interrupted by an interlude of a more serious kind. Just at this time Dr. Solander complained that his pockets had been picked." Of course Captain Cook, in his culpable carelessness of style, had made the simple entry, "Solander had his pocket picked." When we read of the "poetical fables of Arcadia," of the "famous Purpura of the Ancients," we feel the felicity of passing Cook through a classical mill. And what polite ear can endure to be told that the captain "went about with the king" when it is possible to say that "the commander pursued his journey under the auspices of that potentate"? The ship's log, again, should be kept in balanced sentences, witness the following, which forms part of a classical account of a boxing match between two savages: "We observed with pleasure that the conqueror never exulted over the vanquished, and that the vanquished never repined at the success of the conqueror." And the following is a charming illustration of the lofty and refined level on which a sailor's log ought to be maintained: "It is scarcely possible for those who are acquainted with the athletic sports of remote antiquity not to remark a rude resemblance of them in this wrestling match among the natives of a little island in the midst of the Pacific Ocean. And our female readers may recollect the account given of them by Fenelon in his Telemachus, where, though the events are fictitious, the manners of the age are faithfully transcribed from authors by whom they are supposed to have been truly related." All this written by Captain Cook in Matavai Bay! After this it no longer surprises us to hear him reminding us how "Ælian and Apollonius Rhodius impute a certain practice to the ancient inhabitants of Colchis, a country near Pontus in Asia, now called Mingrelia."

In spite of all, the story of Cook's first voyage proved the most interesting account of adventure and discovery ever yet presented to English readers. For the reason already given I do not propose to make long extracts from it. The following is the skeleton course of the ship.

August 26th, 1768. The *Endeavour* set sail from Plymouth Sound.

September 13th. Madeira. The narrative speaks of kindness and hospitality received here. Mr. George Forster darkly hints at a discreet silence being thrown over a certain bombardment of Fort Loo at Madeira by an English man-of-war, assisted by Captain Cook, in revenge for an insult offered to the British flag. Perhaps. Who knows?

November 13th. Rio de Janeiro.

January 14th, 1769. Entered the Strait of Le Maire. The ship doubled Cape Horn and arrived off the western end of the Magellan Strait in thirty-three days, the ship having sustained no damage.

April 10th. Sighted Otaheite, having on the run from Cape Horn discovered several small islands, namely, Lagoon Island, Thurnel Cape, Bow Island, The Groups, Bird Island, and Chain Island.

April 13th. Anchored in Matavai Bay.

June 1st. Transit of Venus successfully observed.

July 13th. Left Otaheite and cruised among the islands of the group, landing on those called by Cook Huaheine, Bolabola, Ulietea, Otaha, Tubai, and Maurua.

October 7th. New Zealand sighted. The whole of the coast of New Zealand was examined, the country being proved to consist of two islands, and to form no part of the great southern continent. Six months were given to this work.

March 31st, 1770. Sailed from New Zealand.

April 28th. Anchored in Botany Bay. Cook then followed up the coast of Australia northward for two thousand miles.

August 25th. Left the coast of New South Wales and steered for the coast of New Guinea. Passed through Torres Strait and established the fact that New Guinea and New Holland are separate islands. Touched at Timor, Savu, and Batavia.

June 12th, 1771. Anchored in the Downs.

The results of this voyage have been summed up as follows by Cook himself in the introduction to his account of the second voyage.

I was ordered to proceed directly to Otaheite, and after astronomical observations should be completed, to prosecute the design of making discoveries in the South Pacific Ocean by proceeding to the south as far as lat. 40°; then if I found no land to proceed to the west between 40° and 35° till I fell in with New Zealand, which I was to explore; and thence to return to England by such route as I should think proper.

In the prosecution of these instructions I sailed from Deptford the 30th July 1768; from Plymouth the 26th of August; touched at Madeira, Rio de Janeiro, and Strait Le Maire, and entered the South Pacific Ocean by Cape Horn in January the following year.

I endeavoured to make a direct course to Otaheite, and in part succeeded; but I made no discovery till I got within the tropic, where I fell in with Lagoon Island, The Groups, Bird Island, Chain Island, and on the 13th of April arrived at Otaheite, where I remained three months, during which time the observations on the transit were taken.

I then left it; discovered and visited the Society Isles and Ohetoroa; thence proceeded to the south till I arrived in lat. 40° 22′ S., long. 147° 29′ W., and on the 6th of October fell in with the east side of New Zealand.

I continued exploring the coast of this country till the 31st of March 1770, when I quitted it and proceeded to New Holland; and having surveyed the eastern coast of that vast country, which part had not before been visited, I passed between its northern extremity and New Guinea, landed on the latter, touched at the island of Savu, Batavia, Cape of Good Hope, and St. Helena, and arrived in England on the 2nd of July 1771.

The publication of the journals of this voyage was looked for with the greatest eagerness. As might be expected, the official narrative was anticipated by productions written hastily and without the maps and charts. One of them was anonymous, the work of some one who had been on board and concealed his name, the other was the journal of Banks's draughtsman, Mr. Sydney Parkinson, a copy of which was obtained surreptitiously. This, which was enriched by Parkinson's drawings, was suppressed by an injunction. Hawkesworth's narrative was not published until after Cook's departure for the second voyage. He asserts, no doubt with perfect truth, that he submitted it to Cook for perusal before he went away, and to Banks before publication. Everything, it is certain, was there; he had omitted no incident either from Cook's or Banks's journals, but the work, as it appeared, belonged neither to Cook nor to Banks.

Apart from the immense body of new geographical work accomplished in the voyage, it is remarkable for having led to a more successful method of treating that terrible scourge of every voyage, scurvy. We have seen how Wallis treated it; in the account of the second voyage we shall see how Cook treated it. But on this, his first voyage, and perhaps his first long voyage, unless we count the passage of the Atlantic a long voyage, he seems to have had no experience of scurvy, and to have taken no special precautions. The experience of Byron, whose company suffered horribly from this scourge, could not have been unknown to him. Byron returned in 1766, two years before the *Endeavour* sailed, and although his journals had not yet been published, the Admiralty had all the information, and could hardly withhold a fact so important as the prostration of half the crew. Nothing, however, is said of special precautions. Moreover, very little is said about scurvy during the first part of the voyage, when they were seldom, after the six weeks' run from Cape Horn to Tahiti, many days from land. On their return voyage, however, after leaving Batavia, where the whole company seemed to have been poisoned by the heat and the stinks of the place, scurvy and fever together fell upon the crew, so that forty were on the sick list. Out of the forty twenty-three died. This dreadful calamity, the sight of all the suffering, impressed Cook so much that in future we shall find him taking as much thought for the prevention of scurvy as for the prosecution of the enterprise in hand; and after the second voyage he was as much congratulated on his success in this respect as on his achievements as an explorer of unknown seas.

The death list, indeed, was frightful. The astronomer, Charles Green, died; the surgeon, Monkhouse, died; the first lieutenant, Hicks, died;

among others who died were Sporing and Parkinson, both of Banks's party; two midshipmen; the master, "a young man of good parts, but unhappily given up to intemperance, which brought on disorders that put an end to his life"; the boatswain; the carpenter, his mate, and two of his crew; the sail maker, a good old man of seventy, who had kept himself from fever in Batavia by getting drunk every day, and his mate; the corporal of marines, the cook, and in all about a dozen seamen. This was a goodly roll out of a company of eighty. But this was the last voyage in which scurvy was to demand such an enormous proportion of victims. Cook was going to prove the best physician ever known in the prevention of scurvy. The only true method of prevention, however, the mode of preserving every variety of fresh food, was not discovered for a long time afterwards. Mr. Clark Russell has remarked in his Life of Dampier that in those days they over-salted the beef and pork. The remark is equally true of the provisions served out in Cook's time. They were over-salted. George Forster, of the second voyage, complains bitterly of the time when the private stores of the officers and passengers were exhausted, and they had to live on the ship's provisions just like the crew. He tells us how, every day, the sight and smell of the salt junk that was served to them made them loathe their food, which, besides, was so hard that there was neither nourishment nor flavour left in it. Imagine the misery, the solid misery, of having to live upon nothing but a fibrous mass of highly-salted animal matter, accompanied by rotten and weevily biscuit! Think of this going on day after day for a hundred days, and sometimes more, at a stretch, three long months, with no bread, vegetables, butter, or fruit; even the water gone bad, and no tea, coffee, or cocoa.

It seems a slight to the memory of Captain Cook to dismiss his first voyage with so scant a notice; but, indeed, Dr. Hawkesworth has taken the commander out of the narrative so completely that nothing remains of him but a shadow who moves and acts; we never catch his eye, we never hear him speak. As the captain, so the company. The followers of Captain Jason himself, or the crew who threw Jonah into the waves, are hardly more shadowy than the crew of the *Endeavour*. We may dismiss this first voyage with one more remark. When a voyage of *Discovery* is sent out in these days, most places are supposed to be so well known as to require no detailed description, though observations may be made on points of new or special interest. This was not so with Cook. He, or Dr. Banks, or Dr. Hawkesworth, thinks it necessary to give descriptions of every place the ship visited. Madeira, the Cape of Good Hope, and Batavia require a description almost as full and complete as Otaheite, New Zealand, and the coast of New Holland.

This is fortunate for us. Many things have been changed since then, especially in Batavia, where, it is hoped, they no longer punish their malefactors by impalement, nor do their ladies flog and torture their female slaves out of jealousy. The colonial government has also, perhaps, learned a little civility and hospitality; and one would like to learn that they have cleaned up the place a little. But the account of that Dutch colony and that of Cape Town are most valuable as contemporary pictures of a kind of life now passed away. Every one who has endeavoured to reconstruct life as it was a hundred or two hundred years ago must know how extraordinarily difficult it is to find records exact and minute. Cook's, or Banks's, or Hawkesworth's notes on Batavia will always be as useful to one considering colonial ways in the last century as to those who study Polynesian manners, customs, language, and tradition at the moment of their *Discovery*. Many stories told of this voyage greatly affected the popular imagination. I have not quoted any of them for reasons already stated. The night of terror and freezing cold spent by Banks and his companions on a hillside of Tierra del Fuego in the height of the Antarctic summer; the soft and gentle manners of the Otaheitans, whose ladies, though not so beautifully dressed, reminded the tender-hearted mariners, in many particulars, of Poll and Doll and Moll, those fair maids of Point and St. Mary Street; the fierce New Zealanders; the vast island of New Holland, so thinly populated, bigger, they said, than the whole of Europe (heavens! what treasures must be waiting in that vast unexplored country); the perils of the *Endeavour* among the coral reefs; the lovely island of Savu; the luxury, the drunkenness, the cruelty, the vice, the heat, the stinks, the fever of Batavia, all these things enlarged the narrow world and filled men with wonder and delight, so that they held out their hands, and with one common consent they called for more.

CHAPTER VII

A BREATHING SPACE

COOK returned home on June 12th, 1771. In his absence, a day or two before he sailed out of Plymouth, a child had been born to him, but it died in infancy. He also learned that his second child, Elizabeth, born in 1766, was dead. His wife was living at Mile End Old Town, a name given both to the few scattered houses along that part of the Mile End Road where is now the People's Palace, and to the houses on the east Side, the old side, of Stepney Green. The house now pointed out as Cook's is No. 88 Mile End Road, a small and rather mean house at present, one of a row of shops. The more respectable residents of the Mile End Road were retired masters of merchant vessels or the grass widows of skippers still in active work.

No one who gets acquainted with the family life of the last century can avoid remarking the great number of children who died. Thus Cook lost four at least of his brothers and sisters in childhood. He also lost three out of six of his own children. Yet his brothers lived in the healthiest part of England, and his children in the open country a mile from Aldgate. His own constitution was of iron, and his wife lived to be more than ninety, so that there was no hereditary weakness.

It would seem, however, as if there was little leisure for anything but business. He had first to put in order, and to deliver to the Admiralty, all his notes, journals, logbooks, and observations, with the drawings and charts.

This done, he might have sat down to rest a while. Perhaps he did, but his power of taking rest was less than that usually granted to man. At all events, he found time to write a paper for the Royal Society, called "An Account of the Flowing of the Tides in the South Sea, as observed on board His Majesty's Bark, the *Endeavour*." This paper, as well as one on the Scientific Results of the Voyage, was published by the Society in their *Philosophical Transactions*.

Cook was promoted to the rank of commander. He hoped, it is said, to have been made a post-captain, but this was not allowed. To us it seems a very small thing whether Cook should rank as a commander or as a post captain; the greatness of a man's achievement is not to be measured by his promotion, or even by the recognition of his own contemporaries, though, in general, a man's own contemporaries generally overestimate the achievements of their leaders, as boys at school think the greatest man in the world is the captain of their eleven. Besides, there is in every age a fashion in the conferring of rank and promotion; in these days we have seen the greatest traveller of the age rewarded after he had reached the age of sixty with a simple knighthood; we have also seen, and it greatly increases our admiration for the national honours, the owners of great incomes created peers; in those days they reserved their peerages first for the men who defeated the French by sea or land, next for the younger sons of noblemen who distinguished themselves as statesmen, and, lastly, for lawyers. The immeasurable importance of the gifts which Cook had bestowed upon his country was such as to require the prophetic gift, the supreme wisdom, to recognise it; and surely there was little of that wisdom in the statesmen of 1770. He had given to his country Australia and New Zealand nothing less; he had given to Great Britain Greater Britain. If people had only suspected or guessed a thousandth part of what was to come out of this voyage, what reward would have been thought too great?

Cook got no title, and, I am quite certain, expected none. He humbly hoped to be made a post-captain, and he had to be contented with a single step. Let us hope that he was satisfied. The man is silent; we cannot tell what he hoped, or whether he was satisfied with what he got; there is only one document of his extant in which he is allowed to say the word he intended, and in that document he says nothing about his hopes or his ambitions.

He was at home this time for exactly a year. But if the beginning of his leave was spent in preparing papers for the Admiralty, the end of it was fully occupied in preparing for another voyage to the same regions. It was a great thing in those days to have put a girdle round the earth; and it was such a painful and laborious thing, so full of discomforts and anxieties, that there were few who cared to attempt the feat a second time.

Meantime the smouldering controversy about the great southern continent began again to rage vehemently. In 1770 appeared the first volume of Dalrymple's Collection of Voyages, which started the dispute afresh.

The recent voyage of Captain Cook had not, it was true, succeeded in finding that continent; on the other hand, he had not looked for it. His discoveries in respect to New Holland and New Zealand did not in the least disprove its existence: they only shifted the ground where it might lie. The believers in the continent were not in the least degree disposed to surrender their Terra Australis Incognita because Cook had not found it. Such a beautiful land, round which had been woven so many pleasing speculations, was not lightly to be abandoned. For two hundred years the southern continent had been believed in; it will be found laid down with much precision on many of the old maps; wherever bits of land, capes, corners, and angles, nay, even islands, were discovered, they were set down on the map as part of the great southern continent. Tasman, for instance, thought that the corner of New Zealand discovered by himself belonged to it. Lozier Bouvet, sent out by the French East India Company in 1738, reported land in lat. 54° S. and long. 11° E. This land, it has never been found by any subsequent traveller, was also concluded to be part of the continent: and early in 1675 an English merchant, Anthony La Roche, being carried out of his course by winds and currents, fell in with a coast now supposed to have been the island of Georgia, which was also concluded to be the southern continent. The discoveries of Quiros again pointed the same way. Given the existence of such a continent, and all these discoveries could be easily connected with it. In fact, they were, and every additional spot of land observed from a ship driven southwards by bad weather became an addition to the coast of the continent.

Dr. Kippis, Cook's biographer, writing in the year 1788, thus speaks of this belief: "The writer of this narrative fully remembers how much his imagination was captivated in the more early part of his life with the hypothesis of a southern continent. He has often dwelt upon it with rapture, and been highly delighted with the authors who contended for its existence, and displayed the mighty consequences which would result from its being discovered. Though his knowledge was infinitely exceeded by that of some able men who had paid a particular attention to the subject, he did not come behind them in the sanguineness of his hopes and expectations." In short, the southern continent was a thing which had grown up in men's minds until, to many who thought and wrote about it, the great unknown land stretched round the whole of the Antarctic Pole; it contained treasures greater than any which had been found in the Americas; it was populated by a race highly civilised, who had acquired a knowledge of the arts; it would be a possession for that European nation which should find and claim it greater and richer than were ever the Spanish dominions in the west. "Its longitude", see Dalrymple's Collection, "is as much as that of all Europe, Asia Minor, and to the Caspian Sea and Persia, with all the islands of the Mediterranean and Ocean which are in its limits embraced, including England and Ireland. That unknown part is a quarter of the whole globe, and so capacious that it may contain in it double the kingdoms and provinces of all those your Majesty is at present lord of, and that without adjoining to Turks or Moors or others of the nations which are accustomed to disquiet and disturb their neighbours."

Dalrymple, himself an ardent advocate of the southern continent, thus dedicates his Historical Collection of Voyages: "To the man who, emulous of Magellan and the heroes of former times, undeterred by difficulties, and unseduced by pleasure, shall persist through every obstacle, and not by chance but by virtue and good conduct succeed in establishing an intercourse with a Southern Continent!"

The Earl of Sandwich, at that time the First Lord of the Admiralty, took a great interest in these questions. It seems to have been chiefly due to him that an expedition was resolved upon which should endeavour to clear up and finally settle the controversy concerning the continent. How far Cook himself was consulted does not appear. In Cook's own words: "Soon after my return in the *Endeavour* it was resolved to equip two ships to complete the *Discovery* of the Southern Hemisphere." That he was consulted as to the conduct and equipment of the expedition is evident from his introduction to the second voyage, in which he discusses, the passage has already been quoted, the kind of vessel most useful for such a voyage, and shows that his advice was acted upon.

It does not appear that there was ever any hesitation on the part of Lord Sandwich as to the proper person to command the new expedition. I know not where Captain Wallis was at this time, or Captain Carteret, but both were passed over and the command was offered to Cook. He accepted it without hesitation.

The date of his commission was November 28th, 1771. The interval of five months was therefore all the time he had to bestow upon his family; and this interval, as we have seen, must have been pretty well occupied with business relating to the last voyage. From the time of his appointment he must have been fully occupied with the preparations and the equipment of his ships, so that the family at Mile End Old Town saw but little of their father. As in the case of the former voyage, a child was born a few days after the departure of the ships ; and, as before, the child died in infancy.

The disasters of the previous voyage caused Cook to take many new precautions against scurvy. He put on board wheat instead of oatmeal, sugar instead of so much oil, and a quantity of malt, sauerkraut, salted cabbage, portable broth, saloop, rob of lemons, mustard, marmalade of carrots, and inspissated juice of wort and beer. Some of these things were experimental, and failed to produce any good effect. Others were well known for their antiscorbutic properties. In fact, for the first time in the history of navigation a carefully prepared attempt was to be made in the prevention of this disease.

When all was ready, the ship sailed from Deptford on April 9th, 1772, but being detained by east winds got no farther than Woolwich, where she lay for a fortnight. She then dropped down to Longreach, but had to put in for repairs at Sheerness. On June 22nd she sailed for Plymouth, and finally quitted Plymouth Sound on July 13th.

CHAPTER VIII

THE SECOND VOYAGE

ONE opens the account of the second voyage with relief and hope. We have done with Dr. Hawkesworth; it is true that we have Dr. Douglas in his place, but the second editor declares solemnly that he has given the very words of the writer without alteration. This is substantially true; there may be omissions, but the language is never altered, nor shall we find inserted any of the "judicious" observations. If anywhere we shall find the man himself in this journal, we shall hear his voice and look into his face and read his mind. Certainly Cook was not brought up in a school which encourages personal confidences and bits of autobiography; we must not expect too much; but we are all human, and except in a Royal Engineer's report, which is written in the third person, a man may discover himself even in a ship's journal or a log-book. One may even discern the character of a clergyman from his manner of keeping a parish register.

When one reads this narrative, it is truly wonderful to understand how any one would have thought of improving Cook's style by subjecting it to the handling of Dr. Hawkesworth. What have balanced periods, turgid ornaments, and becoming sentiments to do with Cook's plain unvarnished narrative? Simplicity and directness never go out of fashion. We read a book of travels to learn what was observed and discovered, not to linger over the sentences, caught by the charm of the words and dwelling on the music of a phrase. Nay, to the charm of literary style the greater part of the world will always remain blind and deaf; they read for what is told, not for the way in which it is told; they want the story. The skilful artist may so employ his charm of language as to make the manner seem part and parcel of the matter, but the story, the story is everything. In such a story as Cook had to tell, the greatest simplicity and the most perfect directness are the most effective and the most desirable qualities. The reader should have no other thought than to learn what he saw and whither he sailed.

Cook's own journal, then, is here presented in his own words. He says simply in his introduction:

And now it may be necessary to say that, as I am on the point of sailing on a third expedition, I leave this account of my last voyage in the hands of some friends, who, in my absence, have kindly accepted the office of correcting the press for me; who are pleased to think that what I have here to relate is better to be given in my own words than in the words of another person; especially as it is a work designed for information and not merely for amusement, in which it is their opinion that candour and fidelity will counterbalance the want of ornament. I shall therefore conclude this introductory discourse with desiring the reader to excuse the inaccuracies of style which doubtless he will frequently meet with in the following narrative, and that, when such occur, he will recollect that it is the production of a man who has not had the advantage of much school education, but who has been constantly at sea from his youth; and though, with the assistance of a few good friends, he has passed through all the stations belonging to a seaman, from an apprentice in the coal trade to a post captain in the Royal Navy, he has had no opportunity of cultivating letters. After this account of myself the public must not expect from me the elegance of a fine writer or the plausibility of a professed bookmaker, but will, I hope, consider me as a plain man, zealously exerting himself in the service of his country, and determined to give the best account he is able of his proceedings.

These words are straightforward, modest, and manly. The writer is not ashamed of having risen from the lowest position possible on a ship; on the other hand, he is prepared to maintain his own ability to set down what he has seen as plainly as if he had had as many opportunities of cultivating letters as the great man who was appointed to revise his simple and direct account.

Besides Cook's own account, we have to illustrate this voyage a description written by George Forster, younger of the two German naturalists who accompanied the expedition, certain "observations" by the elder Forster, and the scientific results detailed by Wallis and Bayley, the two astronomers.

Forster's book, which appeared in 1777, was regarded as a breach of confidence. His father, to whom he was assistant, was sent out as naturalist, with general instructions to make observations of every kind. He also seems to have thought that he would be called upon to write the history of the voyage, to succeed the great Hawkesworth. On his return he still imagined that he would be expected to do this, and actually began it, but found that the captain's journal was to be kept separate from his own. Lord Sandwich, however, undertook to present Cook and Forster with the plates, engraved at the expense of the Admiralty, of all the drawings and maps made during the voyage to accompany the journals; and Forster was informed that he would not be called upon to write the history of the voyage at all, but to send in his observations as they were. Unless he agreed to this, he would forfeit any share in the profits of the work. Here the son saw his chance. He was not bound, he said, by any agreement which his father had made. He therefore wrote his own account of the voyage, and, on the whole, though somewhat flowery and exaggerated, it is a very good book indeed. The Government and Captain Cook, unfortunately, took a different view of his obligations, and, it is said, expressed these views so strongly that the two Forsters found that no further appointments would be offered them, and retired to their native country, where I know not what became of them. The father is said to have been of a turbulent temper: the son grumbled throughout the voyage at the loss of his little comforts; but Cook has no word of complaint against either of them, nor have they any other charge against the captain than that he would persevere with the work before him, though it made his people more uncomfortable every day.

Two ships were chosen and fitted out for this expedition. Both of them were built at Whitby, on much the same lines as the *Endeavour*. They were at the time about fourteen or sixteen months old. One of them, the *Resolution*, was of four hundred and sixty-two tons burden; the other, the *Adventure*, of three hundred and thirty -six tons. The former was fitted out at Deptford, the latter at Woolwich. The *Resolution* carried a company of one hundred and twelve men, the *Adventure* eighty-one. Each ship was provisioned for two years and a half. We have seen how, mindful of his late disasters, Cook carried with him a great quantity of antiscorbutics.

The frame of a small vessel of twenty tons was put on board each ship, to be put together and to serve as tenders on any emergency, such as shipwreck. Both ships were provided with a quantity of things, such as the natives would like, for presents or trade. A number of medals were struck, on one side the king's head, and on the other the two ships. Warm clothing was laid in.

The scientific branch of the expedition was provided for first, by placing an astronomer, provided by the Board of Longitude, with proper instruments in each ship. Mr. Wallis was on the *Resolution*, and Mr. Bayley on the *Adventure*. Mr. William Hodges, a landscape painter, was engaged to make drawings and paintings of places and people; and the two Germans, John Reinhold Forster and his son George Forster, already spoken of, were engaged as skilful in natural history.

The following is a list of the instruments supplied. It may be curious to compare it with such as would now be supplied.

A portable observatory. A dipping needle. Two astronomical clocks. A marine barometer. A transit instrument. A wind gauge. An astronomical quadrant. Two portable barometers. A reflecting telescope of two feet focal length. Six thermometers. A theodolite with a level and a chain. An achromatic refracting telescope of three and a half feet. An apparatus for testing the heat of the sea water at different depths. Two Hadley's sextants. An azimuth compass. A pair of globes. Four timekeepers.

As regards the ship's company, the second and third lieutenants, the lieutenant of marines, two of the warrant officers, and several of the petty officers on the *Resolution* had sailed with Cook on the *Endeavour*. That so many were ready to go with him again shows the confidence they placed in him, as well as his power of attracting the affection of his subordinates. The captain of the *Adventure*, Tobias Furneaux, had been Wallis's first lieutenant.

On July 13th the ships sailed from Plymouth Sound.

My instructions were to make the best of my way to the island of Madeira, there to take in a supply of wine, and then proceed to the Cape of Good Hope, where I was to refresh the ships' companies and to take on board such provisions and necessaries as I might stand in need of. After leaving the Cape of Good Hope, I was to proceed to the southward and endeavour to fall in with Cape Circumcision, which was said by Monsieur Bouvet to lie in lat. 54° S., and in about 11° 20' E. long, from Greenwich. If I discovered this cape, I was to satisfy myself whether it was a part of the continent which had so much engaged the attention of geographers and former navigators, or a part of an island. If it proved to be the former, I was to employ myself diligently in exploring as great an extent of it as I could, and to make such notations thereon, and observations of every kind, as might be useful either to navigation or commerce, or tend to the promotion of natural knowledge. I was also directed to observe the genius, temper, disposition, and number of the inhabitants, if there were any, and endeavour by all possible means to cultivate a friendship and alliance with them; making them presents of such things as they might value, inviting them to traffic, and showing them every kind of civility and regard. I was to continue to employ myself on this service, and making discoveries either eastward or westward, as my situation might render most eligible, keeping in as high a latitude as I could, and prosecuting my discoveries as near to the South Pole as possible, so long as the condition of the ships, the health of their crews, and the state of their provisions would admit of, taking care to reserve as much of the latter as would enable me to reach some known port, where I could procure a sufficiency to bring me home to England. But if Cape Circumcision should prove to be part of an island only, or if I should not be able to find the said cape, I was in the first case to make the necessary survey of the island, and then to stand on to the southward so long as I judged there was a likelihood of falling in with the continent, which I was also to do in the latter case, and then to proceed to the eastward in further search of the said continent, as well as to make discoveries of such islands as might be situated in that unexplored part of the southern hemisphere, keeping in high latitudes, and prosecuting my discoveries as above mentioned as near the pole as possible, until I had circumnavigated the globe, after which I was to proceed to the Cape of Good Hope, and from thence to Spithead.

In the prosecution of these discoveries, wherever the season of the year rendered it unsafe for me to continue in high latitudes, I was to retire to some known place to the northward to refresh my people and refit the ships, and to return again to the southward as soon as the season of the year would admit of it. In all unforeseen cases I was authorised to proceed according to my own discretion; and in case the *Resolution* should be lost or disabled I was to prosecute the voyage on board the *Adventure*.

There is shown at the Museum of Whitby, besides a boat-yoke used by Cook, a so-called model of the *Resolution*. She is a stout vessel, three-masted, broad in the beam, and built for strength before speed, one understands only by looking at her how the ship took one hundred and nine days to get from Plymouth to Table Bay on this voyage, and ninety-nine days on the next. Her figurehead is a black savage with a spear and shield; she has no bulwarks, but, this detail is clearly wrong, a strong timber railing runs round her, leaving her totally unprotected from the breaking of seas over her, which, therefore, would sweep her clean as they now do on the Atlantic steamers; there is no waist and no high stern; her upper deck is nearly flush, the quarter-deck being raised about a foot; there are no cabins or rooms on the upper deck ; and there is no kind of protection for the sailors, so that in rough weather no one except the watch would be able to go on deck at all. A hatchway forward and another aft lead down to the main deck, on which were placed and worked the twenty-six guns for which she was pierced. It appears, however, that the model is inaccurate, because the *Resolution* carried no more than twelve, and was only pierced for sixteen. On the main deck also must have been the workshops, as well as the mess tables, the officers' cabins, and the captain's room. Perhaps the men slung their hammocks here as well. The masts, if the model is faithful, were thick and stout, and so were the yards. One thinks of the company on board this little vessel, one hundred and twelve men all cooped up in this narrow space for a three years' voyage; there were, besides, live stock on board in great numbers to be landed on the islands, bulls, cows, rams, ewes, goats, fowls. Great indeed was the courage of our grandfathers. Smollett has shown us how they lived down below in the darkness and the stench without too much grumbling; but Roderick Random's ship was not provisioned for two years, nor did it carry bulls and cows and sheep and goats. Any one who has ever seen a cattle-boat will appreciate the power of these innocent creatures to create for the sailors a special kind of misery. Perhaps in warm soft climates, when the ports were open and the trade breeze blew gratefully through and through the ship, the men's quarters were fresh and sweet; but when she was plying painfully among the ice-fields of the southern sea; when the ports were closed and the icy breath of the south drove the men below; when the sails were sheets of frozen canvas, and every rope was covered with a thin sheathing of ice; then ... but the crews were accustomed to discomfort; it was only the landsmen on board who made complaint.

We will follow this voyage with the help of Mr. George Forster's book rather than that of the captain's journal, which everybody has read. It is a book in which we hear something of the daily talk among the passengers, if not among the crew; there are details in it which were below the dignity of the captain's journals; we see how those on board liked it who had no enthusiasm for the great southern continent.

July 13th, 1772. Sailed from Plymouth Sound. Touched at Port Praya in the island of St. Jago.

October 30th-November 22nd. Table Bay. Here Herr Sparrman, botanist, and pupil of the great Linne, joined the expedition.

On leaving the Cape the men were served out jackets and trousers of stout flannel called fearnought. Orders were given not to waste the water, and everybody had to wash in salt water. Forster also mentions the discomfort caused by the rough weather, which they got here for the first time. On December 10th they sighted the ice. They were now in the longitude assigned by Bouvet to the headland which he claimed to have seen and named Cape Circumcision, but their latitude was ninety-five miles south of his. So that if they sailed over the land south of that cape, it could not very well belong to a continent. This, in fact, they afterwards did.

For six weeks the ships sailed among icebergs, getting south whenever an opening appeared. Two or three cases of scurvy were declared and cured by copious doses of fresh wort. The crews also took sauerkraut every day and had portable broth. Christmas Day was spent, Forster tells us, with the usual cheerfulness by the officers and passengers, and by the sailors "with savage noise and drunkenness, to which they seem to have particularly devoted the day." The naturalist was greatly affected by the situation in which he found himself. He speaks of "the gloomy uniformity with which we slowly passed dull hours, days, and months, in this desolate part of the world. We were almost perpetually wrapped in thick fogs, beaten with showers of rain, sleet, hail, and snow, surrounded by innumerable islands of ice, against which we daily ran the risk of being shipwrecked, and forced to live upon salt provisions, which concurred with the cold and wet to infect the mass of our blood."

The captain mentions the fog and sleet, and notes that the rigging was ornamented with icicles, but he says nothing about the dull hours ; and what with watching the ice, sending out boats to look for openings, making experiments with his antiscorbutics, and calculating longitudes, he seems to have found the time anything but dull.

At last, however, being in lat. 67° 15' S., to Forster's great joy they came upon such an immense field of ice that the captain concluded to try no more that season and steered north. "Very natural," says Forster, "that our people, exhausted by fatigues and the want of wholesome food, should wish for a place of refreshment, and rejoice to leave a part of the world where they could not expect to meet with it." He says that there were now a good many cases of scurvy on board. The captain, on the contrary, says that there was but one, he means, of course, one case of importance.

"Thus ended," says Forster, when the ship arrived at New Zealand, "our first cruise in the high southern latitudes.... Our whole course from the Cape of Good Hope to New Zealand was a series of hardships which had never been experienced before. All the disagreeable circumstances of the sails and rigging shattered to pieces, the vessel rolling gunwale to, and her upper works torn by the violence of the strain.... We had the perpetual severities of a rigorous climate to cope with. Our seamen and officers were exposed to rain, sleet, hail, and snow; our rigging was constantly encrusted with ice, which cut the hands of those who were obliged to touch it; our provision of fresh water was to be collected in lumps of ice floating on the sea, when the cold and the saline element alternately numbed and scarified our sailors' hands;" and so on. In fact, the ship had sailed into the Antarctic Ocean. The discomforts which the landsman exaggerates into miseries were hardly noticed by the sailors. The voyage was dangerous, but not more disagreeable than Cook had so often experienced, for fog, sleet, and snow off the coast of Labrador. And as for the cold of which Forster complains so much, the thermometer hardly ever sank below freezing point. But this author's main object was to write up the dangers and the miseries he had experienced. Everything was exaggerated with the view of effect.

March 26th, 1773. After a run of three thousand five hundred leagues and a hundred and twenty -two days the ship put in at Dusky Bay, New Zealand. Here they made tea, and a kind of beer, from the leaves of a shrub of the myrtle kind. Cook surveyed the coasts of New Zealand till June 7th, meeting his consort the *Adventure*, from which they had been parted after leaving the Cape in Queen Charlotte Sound. Forster's account of New Zealand and the people is highly picturesque and pleasing.

June 7th. Sailed for Otaheite. On the way scurvy broke out on board the *Adventure*. Sighted several small islands. Arrived at Otaheite on August 16th. Forster gives his pen a fuller freedom over this delightful island. At their approach "faint breezes wafted delicious perfumes from the land and curled the surface of the sea. The mountains rose majestic in various spiry forms. Everything seemed as yet asleep, the morning scarce dawned, and a peaceful shade still rested in the landscape." Never, surely, has any island been more described than Otaheite. The most important part of Wallis's narrative is that given to Otaheite. There are at least four long sections in Cook's three voyages devoted to this island. Forster exhausts himself over it. Gilbert, to whom we shall presently come, can find no words to express his admiration of the place and the people. What is more remarkable is the fact that every one of these accounts is separately and individually interesting. They supplement each other. The following general account of the people by Forster seems to represent the emotion of the writer in recalling a fond memory of the delightful place he would never be privileged to visit again. Scientifically, it is vague.

The men are all well proportioned, and some would have been selected by Phidias or Praxiteles as models of masculine beauty. Their features are sweet and unruffled by violent passions. Their large eyes, their arched eyebrows, and high forehead give a noble air to their heads, which are adorned by strong beards and a comely growth of hair. The Sex, the partners of their felicity, are likewise well formed; their irregular charms win the heart of their countrymen, and their unaffected smiles, and a wish to please, ensure them mutual esteem and love. A kind of happy uniformity runs through the whole life of the Tahitians. They rise with the sun, and hasten to rivers and fountains to perform an ablution equally reviving and cleanly. They pass the morning at work, or walk about till the heat of the day increases, when they retreat to their dwellings or repose under some tufted tree. There they amuse themselves with smoothing their hair and anoint it with fragrant oils; or they blow the flute and sing to it, or listen to the song of the birds. At the hour of noon, or a little later, they go to dinner. After their meals they resume their domestic amusements, during which the flame of mutual affection spreads in every heart, and unites the rising generation with new and tender ties. The lively jest without any ill-nature, the artless tale, the jocund dance, and frugal supper bring in the evening, and another visit to the river concludes the actions of the day. Thus contented with their simple way of life, and placed in a delightful country, they are free from cares and happy in their ignorance,

"Ihr Leben fliesset verborgen

Wie klare Bache durch Blumen dahin."

Sept. 1st. Left Otaheite. Cruised among the other islands of the group. Discovered Hervey's Islands. Visited Middleburg and Amsterdam.

Nov. 3rd. Arrived again at Queen Charlotte Sound.

Nov. 26th. Sailed from New Zealand on the second voyage into the Antarctic Ocean. The captain's account of this voyage reads as if everything was as comfortable and everybody as cheerful as could be desired. Alas! to Forster and his father, and perhaps the learned Dr. Sparrman, things looked very different. There was on board, he admits, little scurvy, and everybody drank quantities of the fresh wort. On the other hand, there was a general languor and a sickly look on every person's countenance, "which threatened us with more dangerous consequences," evidently he was one of those who are always thinking of the more dangerous consequences. "Captain Cook himself was likewise pale and lean and entirely lost his appetite." His father, with twelve others on board, was afflicted with rheumatic pains. "Our situation at present," see how a sailor will hide the truth, the captain says nothing of these dreadful things, "was indeed very dismal even to those who preserved the blessing of health; to the sick, whose crippled limbs were tortured with excessive pain, it was insupportable. The ocean about us had a furious aspect, and seemed incensed at the presumption of a few intruding mortals. A gloomy melancholy air loured on the brows of our shipmates, and a dreadful silence reigned amongst us. Salt meat, our constant diet, was become loathsome to all, even to those who had been bred to a nautical life from their tenderest years. The hour of dinner was hateful to us.... The captain seemed to recover as we advanced to the southward."

On January 30th, 1774, they reached in lat. 71° 10' S., long. 106° 54' W., for the second time, the great southern wall of ice. I do not know whether any better description exists of this barrier than the following, written by the captain himself.

On the 30th, at four o'clock in the morning, we perceived the clouds, over the horizon to the south, to be of an unusual snow-white brightness, which we knew announced our approach to field ice. Soon after it was seen from the top masthead, and at eight o'clock we were close to its edge. It extended east and west far beyond the reach of our sight. In the situation we were in, just the southern half of our horizon was illuminated by the rays of light reflected from the ice to a considerable height. Ninety-seven ice hills were distinctly seen within the field, besides those on the outside, many of them very large, and looking like a ridge of mountains rising one above another till they were lost in the clouds. The outer or northern edge of this immense field was composed of loose or broken ice close packed together, so that it was not possible for anything to enter it. This was about a mile broad, within which was solid ice in one continued compact body. It was rather low and flat (except the hills), but seemed to increase in height as you traced it to the south, in which direction it extended beyond our sight. Such mountains of ice as these, I think, were never seen in the Greenland seas, at least not that I ever heard or read of, so that we cannot draw a comparison between the ice here and there. It must be allowed that these prodigious ice mountains must add such additional weight to the ice fields which enclose them as cannot but make a great difference between the navigating this icy sea and that of Greenland.

I will not say that it was impossible anywhere to get farther to the south; but attempting it would have been a dangerous and rash enterprise, and which, I believe, no man in my situation would have thought of. It was, indeed, my opinion, as well as the opinion of most on board, that this ice extended quite to the pole, or perhaps joined on some land to which it had been fixed from the earliest time, and that it is here, that is, to the south of this parallel, where all the ice we find scattered up and down to the north is first formed, and afterwards broken off by gales of wind or other causes and brought to the north by the currents, which are always found to set in that direction in high latitudes. As we drew near this ice some penguins were heard but none seen; and but few other birds, or anything that could induce us to think any land was near. And yet I think that there must be some to the south behind this ice; but if there is, it can afford no better retreat for birds or any other animals than the ice itself, with which it must be wholly covered. I, who had ambition not only to go farther than any one had been before, but as far as it was possible for man to go, was not sorry at meeting with this interruption, as it in some measure relieved us, at least shortened the dangers and hardships inseparable from the navigation of the southern polar regions. Since, therefore, we could not proceed one inch farther to the south, no other reason need be assigned for my tacking and standing back to the north.

They therefore steered north, the captain's intention being to fix the longitude of Juan Fernandez, and to visit Davis Land or Easter Island. On the way he fell ill of what he calls a bilious colic. After his fashion he disposes of this little event in a dozen lines. Forster, however, makes a great deal more of it, and despite his tendency to "write up" everything, shows very clearly that the captain, tough as he was, was sick nigh unto death. In order to give him what was most necessary for his recovery a dog was killed, and a broth of the fresh meat made for him. The illness of the captain was followed by that of the doctor, but fortunately Easter Island was reached, and fresh food was procured again. This interesting place, with its curious sculptures, some of which are now in the British Museum, is described very well both by Cook himself and by Forster.

Leaving Easter Island the ships visited the Marquesas, whose position Cook desired to fix; discovered Hood's Island and Palliser's Island, and once more arrived at Otaheite, to the renewed joy of all on board. Forster, who was classical, exclaimed,

"Ille terrarum mihi praeter omnes Angulus ridet."

And the old free and easy life which the captain made no attempt to restrain began again, insomuch that, as Forster says, they resembled the happy indolent people whom Ulysses found in Phaeacia, and could apply the poet's lines to themselves with peculiar propriety,

"To dress, to dance, to sing, our sole delight,
The feast or bath by day, and love by night."

On May 15th, 1774, they left this earthly Paradise. In the course of this voyage they visited Huaheine, Howe Island, Rotterdam or Annamooka, discovered by Tasman, and discovered Palmerston Island, Savage Island, Mallicollo, Shepherd's Islands, the Sandwich Islands, Erromango, Tanna Island, New Caledonia, of which they explored the south-west coast, and Norfolk Island, a very considerable and memorable voyage by itself, the particulars of which will be found in the narrative.

On October 17th they sighted New Zealand. On November 10th they sailed from New Zealand, and continued without seeing any land till December 17th.

After giving three weeks to the examination of Staten Land and the islands around it Cook sailed on his third and last attempt to find the southern continent, though with no thought of finding it. He did not find it; he discovered the island of Georgia covered over, in the middle of the Antarctic summer, with ice and snow; he also observed certain headlands, and found an islet or two. Then, as on the two previous occasions, Cook consented to return northwards when he could get no farther south.

He had now completely circumnavigated the globe in or near the Antarctic circle. He had traversed the southern ocean in all directions and had found no southern continent anywhere. He now returned to the Cape, and so home, well satisfied, we may suppose, with his success.

Looking into Forster for the humbler details, we find that during the whole of the last run the crew lived chiefly on the fish which they had salted at New Zealand. The salt beef and pork were so universally loathed, that even the captain himself declared he should never again eat it with any degree of satisfaction. The sauerkraut continued to be used, and the wort was still taken as a preventive. But early in February 1775 the sauerkraut was finished, fortunately not long before the end of the southern exploration. On the morning of Sunday, July 30th, 1775, the ships dropped anchor at Spithead.

It doth not become me (Cook sums up) to say how far the principal objects of our voyage have been obtained. Though it hath not abounded with remarkable events, nor been diversified by sudden transitions of fortune, though my relation of it has been more employed in tracing our course by sea than in recording our observations on shore, this, perhaps, is a circumstance from which the curious reader may infer that the purposes for which we were sent into the Southern Hemisphere were diligently and effectually pursued. Had we found out a continent there we might have been better enabled to gratify curiosity; but we hope our not having found it, after all our persevering researches, will leave less room for future speculations about unknown worlds remaining to be explored.

These are modest words. Let us see what Forster says in conclusion.

Thus, after escaping innumerable dangers and suffering a long series of hardships, we happily completed a voyage that lasted three years and sixteen days, in the course of which, it is computed, we ran over a greater space of sea than any ship ever did before us; since, taking all our tracks together, they form more than thrice the circumference of the globe. We were likewise fortunate enough to lose only four men, three of whom died by accident, and one by a disease which would perhaps have brought him to the grave much sooner had he continued in England. The principal view of our expedition, the travel after a Southern Continent within the bounds of the temperate zone, was fulfilled. We had even searched the frozen seas of the opposite hemisphere, within the Antarctic circle, without meeting with the vast tract of land which had formerly been supposed to exist. At the same time we made another *Discovery* important to science, that nature forms great masses of ice in the midst of the wide ocean, which are destitute of any saline particles, but have all the useful and salubrious properties of the pure element. At other seasons we explored the Pacific Ocean between the tropics and in the temperate zone, and then furnished geographers with new islands, naturalists with plants and birds, and, above all, the friends of mankind with various modifications of human nature.

CHAPTER IX

LAST STAY AT HOME

COOK was now at home again for the last time. A simple sum in addition shows that though he was married for nearly seventeen years, his whole residence at home amounted to no more than four years and four months, out of which must be deducted the time necessary for the outfit of his vessel and all the business of preparing his expeditions.

In his public capacity, however, on his return from the second voyage he received all the honours which it was the fashion of the time to bestow. In these days he would have been made rear-admiral and K.C.B., perhaps G.C.B. He would have been presented to the Queen, he would have read a paper at the Royal Geographical Society, he would have been the lion of the season, he would have been invited to take the chair at a hundred meetings, he would also have been implored by the editors of all the magazines to contribute an article, and after sending in his official report to Government, he would have drawn up a narrative of his voyage to be published on his own account, out of which he would have made a considerable sum of money. A hundred years ago simpler methods obtained. This man, who had done for geography and seamanship more in his voyages than any other man who ever lived since Columbus, was promoted to the rank of post-captain; he was also appointed a captain in Greenwich Hospital, a post which provided for him a retreat for life if he pleased to remain there.

He was also elected Fellow of the Royal Society in February 1776. On the day of his election two papers of his, communicated to the president, Sir John Pringle, were read to the Society. One of these was on the action of the tides along the east coast of New Holland, the other on the preservation of the health of the crew on long voyages.

There can be no doubt that the successful prosecution of this voyage raised Cook to a position of the highest respect in his own country, where a man so seldom becomes a prophet. In other countries, at least in France, Holland, Spain, and Russia, he was regarded as the greatest navigator of all time. It is significant of the general feeling that the gold medal of the Royal Society, which is annually awarded to the best experimental research of the year, was in 1776 bestowed upon Captain Cook for his paper on the preservation of the sailors from scurvy. On the day of presentation he had already sailed. He doubtless knew that the honour was intended for him; he could not hear the oration which the president pronounced upon the occasion.

Cook was now in the forty-eighth year of his age; he had been at sea for thirty-four years. This is a long time of service. No man under fifty had worked harder; no living man had achieved so much; other men had been shipwrecked and cast away; plenty of men had encountered perils of every kind; none so many perils or so various as Captain Cook. He might have hung up his oar; there was a safe haven in which he might rest without loss of honour, or without incurring the slightest blame or the least imputation upon his courage. He had done enough. As for what might remain of life, he could have spent it blamelessly in the snug retreat of Greenwich Hospital with his wife and children; he would have awaited the approach of age with a serene conscience, as one who had run a good race and fought a good fight. He could have walked upon the terrace and seen the ships go up and down, the king's ships sailing out on a new voyage of *Discovery* to encounter the coral reefs of New Holland and the hurricane of the tropics and the ice-fields of the Arctic or Antarctic circles. It would have reminded him of his own two voyages. Then he would have told the old tales again, and recalled the soft airs and gentle folk of far-away Tahiti. Why could he not sit down and rest? Besides, he was now a great gentleman, a post captain in the Royal Navy, he who had once been the collier's ship-boy, everybody's servant, cuffed and kicked and ordered about by every common sailor in the vessel, he who had been born in the farm labourer's cottage, and been taught the criss-cross row by a kind lady out of charity. He now enjoyed the society of the greatest scholars and philosophers of his time, he sat at great men's tables, he was called friend by those, his patrons, to whom under less favourable conditions he would have been a servant. He had conquered fortune; he possessed all that life can give a man. Why not sit down and rest and enjoy these things ? Fame, sufficiency, rank in his profession, and friendship of the best, what more can mortal man desire?

But he could not rest. That habit of incessant work was too deep-seated to be thrown off. Besides, Cook at forty -eight was as young as many men at thirty. He had lived a life so hard and simple; it had been so free from vice or excess of any kind; he was born with a constitution so magnificent, that as yet he felt no touch of age. Besides, he who roves must still be roving; the nomad is easily awakened; he who begins to travel can never afterwards sit still. In this age the man who undertakes one journey to Africa is wedded to that continent for life; in that age he who had once breathed the soft airs of the Pacific must needs go back again. Thus Cook took with him on his second voyage not only men who had been with him on the first, but also men who had been with Wallis. As for himself, he eagerly embraced the chance of making the second voyage, and when he was consulted about finding an officer to command the third his pulse quickened, his blood warmed, and he offered to go yet a third time. The Pacific had been kinder to him than to any previous navigators; she suffered him to go back in safety, once, twice, not a third time. Yet if a vision had been granted to Cook before he volunteered, showing him the fatal and ignoble quarrel in which he was to fall, he would still have persevered, seeing how great would be his name and fame.

The question of the southern continent was finally settled. There would be no more wrangling over that; there was no southern continent, or if there should prove to be one it was more inaccessible than Greenland, more inhospitable than the northern coasts of Labrador. It lay behind vast walls and hills of ice, unmelted and unbroken in the height of summer. If any human beings lived there they must be lower than the Eskimo, more wretched than the Fuegian.

But there was another question, open and disputed. It had been under dispute for two hundred years; only in our own days has it been finally settled, and even now it can hardly be considered wholly cleared up while there remain so many islands whose coasts are as yet unexamined. It was the question of the North-Western passage.

This question belongs as much to this century as to the last or the two preceding. It need not be considered with the detail which the history of *Discovery* in the Pacific Ocean seemed to demand. The search for the North-Western passage is, like many scientific searches, one after a thing either impossible to find or useless when found, the pursuit of which yielded results of quite unexpected and of incalculable value. It was hoped to find a short and easy way of sailing to China and the Far East on the north of the American Continent, and so to avoid the long passage by the Cape of Good Hope. How long and tedious the passage was is proved by the fact that, on the second voyage, Cook was a hundred and twenty days sailing from Madeira to the Cape. The expeditions sent out in the sixteenth and seventeenth centuries failed, it is true, to find the passage; but they succeeded in revealing an immense amount of territory in America and a great portion of her northern shores.

In the middle of the eighteenth century the subject was revived, especially by one Dobbs. In the year 1741 Captain Middleton was sent out, and in 1746 Captains Smith and Moore. An Act of Parliament was passed offering a reward of £20,000 to the owners of a ship which should discover the passage, or to the captain, officers, and company of the fortunate ship if it should belong to the Royal Navy. Lord Mulgrave also attempted in the year 1773 to reach the North Pole.

The continual failure of every expedition caused a change of plans. It was then argued that where ships had failed to get through from the Atlantic to the Pacific they might succeed from the Pacific to the Atlantic; and Lord Sandwich was so far persuaded that an attempt in this direction might prove successful that he consented to send out an expedition with this object. Captain Cook would have been appointed to the command without the least hesitation, but for a natural feeling that he had done enough and should now be left to repose. However, whether with the view of sounding him or whether only to consult him, he was invited to dine with Lord Sandwich, and with him were invited his old friends and patrons, Sir Hugh Palliser and Mr. Stephens, Secretary of the Admiralty. During dinner the conversation turned upon the projected expedition, its importance, its dangers, and the benefits which might follow upon its success. Fired once more by the enthusiasm of the navigator, Cook sprang to his feet and offered to take the command. His offer was accepted, with the promise that on his return he should be reappointed to his place at Greenwich Hospital.

One domestic detail of this time survives. Cook concealed from his wife so long as he could the fact that he had promised to try fortune yet once more on the Pacific Main. How long he could keep the thing a secret one cannot learn; as he received his commission in February and began at once to enter men, it could not have been long. Yet to the end his widow lamented that his acceptance of the command had been kept from her. Considering that his youngest child, Hugh, was born just after the ship sailed he may have thought there was good reason not to agitate his wife with any anxieties, but to break the news to her when the whole business was settled.

It is not certain whether he had by this time taken up his official residence in Greenwich Hospital, or whether his wife and family continued to live there until the fatal news arrived. Perhaps they went on living in Mile End Old Town. From recollections preserved by his widow of dinners at great houses during this last stay at home, it would seem as if they had now left that modest suburb.

CHAPTER X

THE THIRD VOYAGE

THE *Resolution* was again chosen for the voyage, and with her the *Discovery* of three hundred tons. Clerke, second lieutenant in the former voyage, was put in command of the smaller vessel. Others who had already sailed with Cook joined this expedition, among them Anderson, surgeon and naturalist, who proved to be the most minute observer and the best linguist of the company; Lieutenant King, who afterwards succeeded to the command of the *Discovery*, and had charge of the astronomical and nautical instruments on board the *Resolution*; while Mr. Bayley, who had been on the second voyage, again went out on board the *Discovery* as astronomer. Several of the petty officers had also sailed on the second voyage. There were more officers in proportion than was usual in a ship of the Royal Navy, the *Resolution* had three lieutenants, the *Discovery* two, and other officers in proportion. This was a practice commonly observed in long and dangerous voyages, partly with the view of easily putting down any attempt at mutiny. Cook, however, states that he brought with him officers for the special service of constructing charts, taking views of coasts and headlands, and drawing surveys of bays and harbours. An artist, Webber, went with them to make drawings of the places where they should touch. The best known portrait of Cook is by Webber. Omai, the Tahitian, who had been brought to England in the last voyage, also went with Cook, to be landed on his native shore; he was laden with presents of all kinds. In respect of wages the ships were put upon the establishments of sloops of war.

As for the sailing instructions they may be summed up in general terms. The commander was to find a northeast passage from the Pacific to the Atlantic if possible. He was also to get together every kind of information in geography in tides, currents, shoals, rocks, harbours, depths, and soundings; natural productions, fruits, grains, minerals, metals, and people. He was also to take possession, "with the consent of the natives," a charming touch of official hypocrisy, in the name of the King of Great Britain and Ireland, of convenient situations in such countries as may be discovered, and so on.

With these instructions and fully equipped the expedition set sail from Plymouth Sound on July 11th.

The following is the skeleton route of this voyage.

Feb. 6th, 1776. Commission to command the *Resolution* received by Captain Cook. He went on board and began to enter men. The *Discovery*, three hundred tons, also purchased, and command given to Captain Clerke.

May 29th. Sailed to Long Reach.

June 25th. Weighed anchor, and made sail for the Downs.

July 11th. Sailed from Plymouth.

Aug. 1st-4th. Teneriffe.

Oct. 18th-Nov. 30th. Table Bay.

Dec. 12th. Islands discovered by Marion and Crozet named by Cook Prince Edward Island, Marion's and Crozet's Islands.

Dec. 24th-30th. Kerguelen Island, Christmas Harbour, examined and explored.

Jan. 24th, 1777. Van Diemen's Land (Adventure Bay).

Feb. 10th. New Zealand.

Feb. 11th-25th. Queen Charlotte Sound.

Feb. 29th. Mangeea Island discovered and visited.

April 1st. Wateea discovered and visited.

April 4th. Wenoo Ette discovered and visited.

April 6th. Hervey's Island visited.

April 13th. Palmerston Island found to be a group of small islets.

April 24th. Passed Savage Island.

April 28th. Annamango, Komango, and Fallafajuca.

April 29th. Annamooka (Friendly Islands).

May 17th. Hepaee.

May 21st. Lefooga (Friendly Islands to nearly due south).

May 22nd. Tongataboo.

Aug. 12th. Tahiti

Sept. 30th Eimeo

Oct. 12th. Huaheme

Dec. 8th. Bolabola

Jan. 20th, 1778. Atooi and Oneeheow (Sandwich Islands).

March 7th. Coast of America.

April 24th. Nootka Sound.

May 11th. Kaye's Island.

June 19th. Selinmagin's Islands.

June 27th. Oonalashka.

Aug. 3rd. Death of Anderson, surgeon and naturalist.

July 9th. Cape Prince of Wales most westerly point of North America. Spent July chiefly in sailing about open sea beyond Behring Straits. Corporal Lidiard, see note, p. 440 in Kippis.

Oct. 26th. Sailed for Sandwich Islands.

Nov. 26th. Discovered Maui.

Nov. 30th. Discovered Hawaii.

Feb. 14th, 1779. Cook killed.

Aug. 2nd. Clerke died of consumption.

Gore took command of the *Resolution*.

King of the *Discovery*.

Oct. 4th, 1780. Arrived at the Nore.

During the voyage the *Resolution* lost five men by sickness, three of whom were ill at start. The *Discovery* lost none.

The account of this voyage, from which the two captains never returned, was published in three volumes quarto, the first and second from the log-books and journals of Captain Cook, and the third by Captain King, who succeeded Captain Clerke in command of the Discovery. Dr. Douglas, Bishop of Salisbury, edited the work. Unfortunately he also doctored it, and though he says in his introduction that Cook's journal was faithfully adhered to, he also owns to incorporating a quantity of matter from Anderson's journal. To prevent the possibility of mistake the editor submitted the first two volumes to King, who was entirely responsible for the third. "All that the editor has to answer for are the notes occasionally introduced in the course of the two volumes contributed by Captain Cook, and the introduction." It is, however, quite clear that many portions of the work have been rewritten or touched, not, it is true, in the lumbering style of Dr. Hawkesworth, but still touched. The straightforward directness and simplicity of Cook's own narrative of the second voyage are gone. The venerable and learned bishop could not understand that it was his religious duty to present the very words of the dead navigator. These given without alteration, he was at liberty to add what notes he pleased, and to enrich the work with Anderson's observations, which are certainly admirable, but not to incorporate them with the body of the work, so that the reader is dragged from Cook to Anderson and from Anderson to Cook. The editor afterwards acknowledges also that Captain King gave advice and directions in a variety of instances when the journal required explanations. Lieutenant Roberts was also " frequently consulted," and particular obligations are due to Mr. Wallis, who "cheerfully took upon himself the trouble of digesting from the log-books the tables of the route of the ships." One Mr. Wegg also assisted, and the Honourable Mr. Davies Barrington and Mr. Tennant and Mr. Bryant, who "followed Captain Cook in his study." In fact, a large number of eminent hands assisted in the production of the work, and if, after so much assistance, there is still much of the original journal left, we ought to be thankful to the editor.

I have before me, however, a journal of the voyage, which has never before been published, kept by George Gilbert of the *Resolution*. He appears to have gone out as master's mate or midshipman on board the *Discovery*. By the successive deaths of Captain Cook and Captain Clerke he was promoted to be lieutenant. George Gilbert's father had been master on the *Endeavour* during the first voyage, and on the *Resolution* during the second. He retired from active service, and lived at Fareham in Hampshire to the age of ninety-one. His son, who on the return of the expedition received promotion, died of smallpox immediately afterwards. The journal fell into the possession of the late Dr. Doran, whose wife belonged to the Gilbert family. It has been most kindly lent to me, with permission to use it for this volume, by Mr. Alban Doran. Many details of interest which are omitted in the official journals have been preserved in this log. I propose to follow the voyage, the route of which has been given above, with the assistance of Mr. Gilbert of the *Resolution*, partly because Cook's own account, as we have seen, has been so much edited, and partly because this narrative is at least new, while Cook's, doctored by the bishop and his friends, has been in the hands of the world for a hundred years.

All the voyages of the latter half of the last century, as I have already said, lie on the borderland between the ancient and the modern. We are as yet too near the navigators of the time to feel the charm of adventure as we feel it in the voyages of Drake and Raleigh, or later in those of Dampier. They belong to a trying period in the history of a book of travel; a hundred years more and Cook will have become, as he really was, the last of the old navigators, the successor, the last, in the long list of Magellan, Tasman, Quiros, Drake, and the rest. A hundred years more and Cook's descriptions of the Polynesians and Australians will be invaluable as a record of things long since passed away; even the people of the islands will have disappeared; there will not be a single survivor of the Friendly Islanders, or of the gentle natives of Tahiti, or of the fierce warriors of New Zealand.

As for information or observation on the manners and customs of the natives, Gilbert's journal affords little or none that is new. On the contrary, his remarks concerning them are of the briefest; evidently he, and with him the great body of the officers, had no training as to the value of such observations or the method of making them. Anderson, for instance, furnishes many pages on the Tasmanians and has put together a short vocabulary of their language. Gilbert sums them up quite in the proverbial style: they wear no clothes and are not ashamed, they know no arts, "except the natives of Terra del Fuego, they are supposed to be the most ignorant race of people existing," which is quite enough attention for a British officer to bestow upon these people.

Let us run through the journal and select those passages which supplement and illustrate Cook and King, and throw light on the daily life and conversation of the officers and men.

At Queen Charlotte Sound the New Zealanders could hardly be persuaded to come on board, probably in fear of retaliation for the murder of the *Adventure*'s men three years before. "I think," says Gilbert, "that nothing can be a greater proof of their treachery than their suspecting it in us." In Cook's account we presently read that he went ashore with a party of men in five boats to collect food for the cattle. The reason for this exhibition of strength is thus given in Gilbert's log. The spelling of the gallant officer is preserved in this extract, but modernised in those that follow.

A boat was sent every day to different parts of the Sound with 8 or 10 people to cut grass for the cattle; I was in that party and it was lucky for us that we never met with any of the Natives for tho' we had arms with us yet they might have rush'd from the woods and cut us off the ship not being able to give us any assistance. One day when we were at Long Island a quarrel happen'd at the ship with the Natives when an old man came on board and told Capt. Cook that some of his countrymen had a design upon our boat; at the same time they saw 3 or 4 large Canoes full of men going over to where the boat was; sent from the ship man'd and arm'd to bring us intelligence and see whether any thing had happen'd; She arrived in time for we had seen nothing of the Natives but however we were order'd to come on board. The next day Capt. Cook made an excursion up the sound with 5 boats and 50 or 60 men well arm'd to cut grass we went up about 12 miles and cut two boat loads on our return we put into Grass Cove the place where the adventures boats crew (consisting of a mate a midshipman and 8 men) were cut off and eat upon the spot by the Natives. No place could be more favourable for such intentions; as the wood was so thick that the Natives could approach close to them before they were discover'd. We saw 4 or 5 of them, who seeing our numbers were afraid to come near us till we made them to understand we had no intentions to hurt them. We had reasons to believe there were a great number of them in the woods as those with us frequently call'd to them; we return'd to the ship that night.

A long and pleasing account of Annamooka or Rotterdam Island is found in Cook's journal. The following sketch of the same place from Gilbert's log is equally pleasing, and more enthusiastic. It also gives us important facts as to the provisioning of the crews.

On the 1st of May came to an anchor at Annamooka, so called by the natives, but by Tasman Rotterdam. This island is low and about six miles in extent, with a lagoon of salt water in the middle of it; and is in my opinion the most delightful spot in the world; being covered with a variety of trees and bushes, forming the most shady and agreeable walks I ever met with. We moored here in twelve fathom water, the bottom rather rocky about half a mile from a sandy beach. The natives came on board in great numbers and behaved in the most friendly manner, being very much rejoiced at seeing the ships again; they brought on board hogs, fowls, and fruit in great plenty; which we purchased of them for hatchets, nails, and beads; every species of the ship's provisions was from this time stopped, and we lived entirely upon the productions of the islands, which was very agreeable to us; sent our tents on shore and the observatories with the astronomers' instruments, for making observations, to regulate our time keeper: had a guard of marines on shore for their protection; sent the cattle on shore for some refreshments, which they were much in want of, being reduced very low. The *Discovery* had both her cables cut through by the coral rocks: she was lucky enough to get both her anchors again, after great trouble. Hove our cables in to examine them, but found them not in the least damaged: had parties on shore cutting wood and watering from a small pond about a quarter of a mile above the beach, which was muddy and brackish, and the only water we could get; but the milk of the cocoa-nuts in a great measure made up for the badness of it: as they were so plentiful we seldom drank anything else; as we secured more hogs here than were sufficient for present use, we began, to salt pork for to carry to sea.

At the Friendly Islands Gilbert gives us a little illustration of that hastiness of temper which is mentioned by all those who speak of Cook's personal character. The incident is not found in the journal.

This isle, which is by far the largest in the cluster, is about seven leagues in length and five in breadth: it is throughout low and level, with the same appearance as the others; we observed part of an eclipse of the sun here. The two chiefs mentioned before came with us and behaved in the most friendly manner imaginable; and supplied the two ships with provisions in great plenty; in all their proceeding they showed a noble, generous, and disinterested spirit; and though their manners were rude and unpolished, yet in every action they displayed an elevation of the mind that would do honour to an European in the most distinguished sphere in life. Played off some fireworks here, which were viewed by a numerous assembly, with acclamations of admiration and surprise. These Indians are very dexterous at thieving, and as they were permitted to come on board the ship in great numbers, they stole several things from us. This vice, which is very prevalent here, Captain Cook punished in a manner rather unbecoming of an European, viz. by cutting off their ears, firing at them with small shot or ball as they were swimming or paddling to the shore, and suffering the people (as he rowed after them) to beat them with the oars and stick the boat-hook into them wherever they could hit them; one in particular he punished by ordering one of our people to make two cuts upon his arm to the bone, one across the other close below his shoulder; which was an act that I cannot account for any other way than to have proceeded from a momentary fit of anger, as it certainly was not in the least premeditated.

And on another occasion he relates an anecdote which shows the courage of the captain. It also illustrates his modesty, as will be seen.

This is what is recorded in the journal.

One of my people, walking a very little way, was surrounded by twenty or thirty of the natives, who knocked him down and stripped him of everything he had upon his back. On hearing of this I seized two canoes and a large hog and insisted on Taoofa's causing the clothes to be restored, and on the offenders being delivered up to me.

This, however, is Gilbert's account of the adventure.

One day when Captain Cook was on shore with a party trading for provisions, having nothing with him but his hanger and a fowling-piece that one of the officers had brought on shore, one of our people separated from the rest, and went up about half a mile into the country, where he was met by the natives, who robbed him of everything, then ran away and left him naked; they at the same time had a very strong inclination to attack the whole party; which Captain Cook perceiving, sent on board for arms, and by a resolute and undaunted courage prevented.

Gilbert's account of the Friendly Islanders, among whom the *Resolution* spent between two and three months, is interesting, but adds little to what we already possess in the captain's journal. Perhaps there is a little more feeling for the sex discovered in the remarks of the younger man.

Although the women have something masculine in their appearance, yet their countenances are pleasing, and their dispositions very mild and agreeable; their dress consists only of a piece of cloth wrapped round their waist, reaching to the knees, in which they are exceeding neat and clean, as well as in their persons: they are always full of mirth and vivacity, and very fond of singing and dancing. . . . The women here, though not so fair as in general in the Society Islands, yet are quite as agreeable, if not more so: their features are regular and beautiful, their mien graceful, both in their persons and dress neat, their dispositions mild and cheerful, and their whole study and endeavour to render themselves pleasing to every one: they seem to be fonder of singing and dancing in their own mode than any girls we have ever seen: and notwithstanding there is a great degree of wantonness in both, yet it is attended with a peculiar kind of simplicity and innocence which, joined to the customs of the country, entirely removes every idea that can be turned to their prejudice. In fact, so pleasing is their temper, so great their vivacity, that even a hermit could not help being delighted with them.

The arrival and stay at Tahiti, which occupy many chapters in Cook and King, are dismissed by Gilbert in four or five pages. He notes the fact that the goats left on the former visit had increased in number and appeared to be thriving. He mentions the visit of the Spanish ship since their last stay, on which Cook has a great deal to say; he describes the canoes of the people, and he is struck with the barbarity of the human sacrifice at which, that is to say, at that part which came after the slaughter of the victim, Cook was present.

At Eimeo happened the incident of the stolen goat. And it really would seem as if the captain on this occasion, too, allowed himself to be carried away by temper. First, the chief Mahein begged a pair of goats, which the captain thought he could not spare unless at the expense of other lands where they might with greater advantage be put ashore. Therefore he refused. The day after, a goat sent on shore to graze was stolen. The goat was brought back the next day; but another, a she-goat, big with kid, was stolen on that very morning. The captain sent a boat after it, but the people pretended to send after it, and amused the petty officers in charge of the boat till the evening.

Next day, according to his own account, Cook led in person a party of men across the island, while Lieutenant Williamson took three boats round to the other side in order to meet him. On the way he called upon all the people to produce the goat, but they denied all knowledge of the animal. "I set fire to six or eight houses, which were presently consumed, with two or three war canoes that lay contiguous to them.

This done, I marched off to join the boats, which were about seven or eight miles from us; and on our way we burned six more war canoes." Next day he broke up, he says, more war canoes, and threatened not to leave a single canoe on the island unless the goat was restored. In the evening the goat was brought back. "Thus ended this troublesome and rather unfortunate business, which could not be more regretted on the part of the natives than it was on mine."

Now hear Gilbert's account of the same unfortunate affair.

The natives having stolen a small goat from us, and not returning it on Captain Cook's demanding it back, the next morning he set out with the marines of both ships and some gentlemen, in all about 35 people well armed, and marched across part of the island in search of it; likewise three boats were sent manned and armed round to meet him during this excursion. Wherever Captain Cook met with any houses or canoes, that belonged to the party which he was informed had stolen the goat, he ordered them to be burnt, and seemed to be very rigid in the performance of his orders, which every one executed with the greatest reluctance except Omai, who was very officious in this business, and wanted to fire upon the natives; but as they every way fled and left their all to the mercy of the destroyers, none of them were killed or hurt; which in all probability they would have been, had they made the least resistance; several women and old men still remained by the houses, whose lamentations were very great, but all their tears and entreaties could not move Captain Cook to desist in the smallest degree from those cruel ravages; which he continued till the evening, when he joined the boats and returned on board, having burnt and destroyed about twelve houses and as many canoes, part of the planks he brought away with him. The next morning he went round again with three boats, where he completed the devastation he had left undone the day before; and all about such a trifle as a small goat, which was that evening brought on board by the natives. I can't well account for Captain Cook's proceedings on this occasion, as they were so very different from his conduct in like cases in his former voyages; if anything may be offered in favour of them, it was his great friendship for Otoo (King of Otaheite), to whom these people were professed enemies.

At the island of Huaheine, also one of the Friendly group, Omai was left ashore. Gilbert's narrative of this business, the landing of the two New Zealanders and the affair of the two deserters, shows the feeling in the ward-room on these events. It was not always, as has already been seen, that of unmixed admiration of the captain's conduct.

Omai, though generally understood to have been brought from Otaheite, was in reality a native of this island; and now chose to make it the place of his residence in preference to any other island in the cluster; accordingly all our carpenters were set to work to build him a house of the planks of the canoes destroyed at Eimeo; which in about a fortnight they completed. His principal furniture was a bed in the English fashion, several tin pots and kettles, and a hand organ, on which he used to play and divert the natives; he had likewise a brace of pistols and a musket, for which we left him a small keg of gunpowder; we also left him a horse and a mare, for which he had a saddle and bridle, and understood the management of them very well. Captain Cook purchased a small space of land round his house for him from the chief, and planned out a garden, in which we sowed several kinds of seeds that we brought out with us, and planted some vines brought from the Cape of Good Hope, which seemed to prosper very well till they were plucked up in the night by some of the natives, for which one of them was the next day brought on board, had his ears cut off, and was kept in irons on the quarter-deck. After he had been in confinement about a week, some of our people took pity on him and released him in the night, so that he made his escape; Captain Cook was exceedingly angry on this occasion, but could by no means find out the person that did it. The two boys that we brought with us from New Zealand were left here as servants to Omai; it is almost impossible to conceive their distress at being forced to part from us, it being entirely against their inclinations to stay here, as it was their earnest desire to go with us to England, but that Captain Cook would not permit; they had now become so well reconciled to us, as not to have the least desire to return to their own country. The oldest, whom

I mentioned before to be the son of a chief, behaved in a manner that gained him the love and esteem of every one in all his actions he displayed a nobleness of spirit above the common rank of people, and never associated with the sailors, but always kept with the gentlemen. He was very sensible and of a mild humane disposition, and had acquired a just abhorrence of the barbarous practices of his countrymen. The youngest was always full of mirth and good humour, and, for his mimicry and other little sportive tricks, was the delight of the whole ship's company. So great was his desire to remain with us that he was obliged to be tied down in the canoe that carried him on shore, having leaped out of it once and attempted to swim back to the ship; the other bore it with a becoming fortitude, disdaining to ask Captain Cook for what he knew he would not grant. They were exceedingly fond of each other, and everybody was sorry to part with them. Omai took his leave of us in a very affectionate manner, and I believe would have been very glad to come back to England; but he knew Captain Cook would not permit him; for the curiosity of the people of England having quite subsided, they began to think him rather a burden on the public, and were glad thus to get clear of him. He was certainly as stupid a fellow as any on the island, and originally of the very lowest degree. Therefore I make no doubt but that he will in a short time be plundered of everything he has, and be forced to return to his former state; but I have not the least idea of their offering him any kind of violence. It may be wondered why the cattle left with the King of Otaheite were not in preference given to Omai; but the reason is very obvious; for as we expect everything to be taken from him, the cattle would but induce the natives to do it sooner, and most probably would be the cause of great contentions among the chiefs before they could agree who were to have them, and perhaps they would be destroyed to put an end to the disputes, as was done in a similar case that we met with afterwards. But should they not be hurt, yet it is most likely that they would be divided among the chiefs, and ever afterward kept separated, which would equally destroy the grand object of forming a breed at these islands: but now they are perfectly free from those dangers as being in possession of the principal person of this country. As for the horse and mare left with Omai, they are not of that consequence as the cattle, therefore it is no great matter what becomes of them. Just before we sailed Captain Cook particularly desired Omai, after we had been gone about three weeks, to send a canoe to us, to the island we were going to; and if the natives treated him ill, to send a black bead, if moderate a blue one, and if well a white one ; which advice he carefully observed. After about a month's stay here we sailed for Ulietea, which lies eight or nine leagues to the westward; and the next morning came to an anchor in Ohamaneno Harbour, on the lee-side of the island. The entrance is between two reefs, and very narrow. Warped up about two miles into a cove at the head of the harbour, hauled the ship close to the shore, and secured her with hawsers to the trees, not being above ten or twelve fathoms from the beach. This island is of a moderate height, and very fertile; it is larger than Huaheine, though small in comparison with Otaheite, and is partly joined by a reef of shoal water upon it to an island about four miles distance called Otahare. The natives here are numerous, and supplied us with provisions in a very plentiful and friendly manner. Sent our observatories on shore as usual; a few days after we had been in, one of our marines, who was placed as a sentinel over the observatories, was found in the night to have quitted his post and gone with his musket into the country. In the morning the sergeant and four marines were sent in search of him, but returned in the evening without getting any intelligence of him. The next morning Captain Cook went in quest of him with two boats armed, and in the afternoon found him amongst a great number of the natives, a few miles from the harbour. He was brought on board and punished with two dozen lashes. A little time after this a midshipman and a common sailor ran away from the Discovery in the night; in the morning, when Captain Cook was informed of it, he went with some boats armed in search of them, and had recourse to his usual practice on these occasions, viz. of inviting some of the chiefs on board, and then confining them till the natives had made full restitution for whatever they had been guilty of; which was always found to have the desired effect, and was certainly the best method that could possibly be taken in these cases to avoid bloodshed; being in general very easily accomplished, as the chiefs usually came on board of their own accord two or three times a day for their amusement. In the present case Captain Clerke was ordered to get the son of Ohan, the king of the island, likewise his daughter and her husband, on board the *Discovery*, and confine them there, which was accordingly done, and the king was told that they should never be released till our two deserters were brought back. He seemed to be greatly distressed on the occasion, and immediately set about making inquiries after them. Captain Cook returned in the evening without getting any intelligence of them; the next morning he set out again, but likewise returned without success; therefore he went no more in quest of them, but depended upon the king's bringing them back. During the confinement of the princes a great number of women came round the ship, and presented a very affecting scene of lamentation by tearing their hair and striking their heads with a shark's tooth that they had in each hand for that purpose, till the blood ran in a continual stream from every part of it. In this manner those Indians express their grief when any great misfortunes befall them; and in the present case there appeared to be an emulation amongst them who should carry it on to the greatest height, till the scene became too moving to be beheld. One afternoon a girl that had followed us from Eimeo informed us that the natives were then going to seize Captain Clerke and Lieutenant Gore, who were on shore together, by way of retaliation for the confinement of their chiefs. Immediately the alarm was given; we were all under arms in an instant; some were sent on shore in quest of Captain Clerke, while others went in the boats along shore to seize all canoes, and to fire upon the natives wherever they saw any, to prevent them assembling together. The people that went in search of Captain Clerke and Mr. Gore found them together before the natives had time to form an attempt; which they certainly intended; for three or four of them, that were with Captain Clerke all the time he was on shore, strove very much to persuade him and Mr. Gore to go into a pool of water they were standing by to bathe (where all of us frequently went for that purpose), which they intended to do; but seeing the natives so very anxious about it, they began to have some suspicion and declined it. Upon this they began to be rather troublesome; till Captain Clerke presented a pistol at them, that he luckily chanced to have with him, which kept them quiet. Our people coming up armed a little afterwards prevented any mischief, and they returned on board safe just before the alarm. Captain Cook, who was on shore close to the ship, was likewise persuaded to go and bathe at the same place, which is nearly a mile distance, but fortunately chanced to refuse; which I think plainly proves that the natives intended to assemble there and to seize them as they were bathing, and carry them off, which by the timely intelligence we received was prevented without any bloodshed.

Our two deserters were brought back after they had been away about a week: they had gone over in a canoe to Bolabola, and from thence to a small island called Tabia, twelve leagues distance from hence, where the natives surprised them when they were asleep, and brought them on board; they were kept in confinement during our stay at these islands. It was well for the natives that they delivered them up so soon, for Captain Cook would very shortly have proceeded to the greatest extremities in his power to get them back, being fully determined not to suffer any person to remain here. Indeed, had he once made a precedent of it, so very flattering was every hope of the great pleasure and happiness to be enjoyed at these islands, together with the many hardships we had to encounter after we left them, that a great part of our people would certainly have deserted us, which would effectually have put a stop to our future proceedings. The natives have always been extremely anxious for some of us to stay with them, and would certainly have detained the deserters and treated them with great friendship and hospitality, had they not been obliged to deliver them up to release their own chiefs. They bore their confinement (which was that of not being allowed to go out of the Captain's cabin) with great fortitude and cheerfulness, and seemingly without the least apprehensions of fear for their situation, which was rendered as agreeable to them as circumstances could possibly admit of. About three or four weeks after we had been here, a canoe arrived from Omai which brought a white bead; which shows that he was still treated in a friendly manner. It is somewhat surprising that the Indian who had his ears cut off at Huaheine for plucking the vines up in Omai's garden, and was kept in confinement on board for some time, till he was suffered to make his escape, should have the confidence to appear here in public alongside the ship, and seemingly without the least fear of being brought on board to his former confinement. Captain Cook, who certainly must have seen him, took not the least notice of him.

On leaving these islands Gilbert, after a short account of the people and their customs, which is of course far better done by his commander and by Anderson, expresses the grief of the ship's company at leaving them. "We left these islands," he says, "with the greatest regret imaginable: as supposing all the pleasures of the voyage to be now at an end: having nothing to expect in future but excess of cold, hunger, and every kind of hardship and distress attending a sea life in general, and these voyages in particular, the idea of which rendered us quite dejected."

There was yet, however, an interval of time before the excess of cold should begin. Meantime they had enjoyed an eight months' respite from the ship's fare, and so long as the plantains held out and fish could be caught they still abstained from the biscuit and the salt junk. "This great supply," says Gilbert, "not only refreshed and strengthened us as much as if we had just left England, but enabled us to prosecute our discoveries northward a second season, and was in a great measure a compensation for that we lost in not being able to fetch Tahiti the first time."

The discovery of the Sandwich Islands completed this voyage across the Pacific from south to north. The chapter in the history, whether by Cook or by Anderson, on the islanders of the archipelago is perhaps the most curious part of the narrative. Gilbert confines himself to the immediate usefulness of the islands, which furnished yams that lasted for a fortnight after their departure.

After that we were put to two-thirds allowance of bread, and had the pork served that we had salted at the Society Islands, which lasted out the greatest part of the season and kept very good all the time. We were allowed a small quantity of sauerkraut, twice a week, to eat with our salt provisions; it is an excellent antiscorbutic, and kept exceedingly well all the voyage. We had likewise portable soup, three times a week, boiled with our peas; which were much the worst article of provisions we had on board; for they had been kiln-dried to keep them, which almost rendered them useless: for after being in the copper six hours they were very little softer than at first, and only just tinged the water they were boiled in. We found the cold to increase very fast as we advanced to the northwards; and hunger accompanying it; for our allowance of bread was very short, and we had no flour served in lieu of beef, which was grown very bad.

The summer of this year was spent in carrying out the main purpose of the voyage, namely, the search for a north-east passage from the Pacific to the Atlantic. A good deal of time was necessarily wasted in repairing the ships, for which purpose King George Sound offered an excellent natural harbour. Here they found a large number of the natives, who brought skins in great quantities for sale, in barter taking in exchange anything of metal, but beads and cloth had no attractions for them. Gilbert, as usual, adds his little homely details.

We purchased several of the dried skins of these animals from the natives, who have them in great plenty; particularly those of the land and sea beavers, but of the two the latter is the most plentiful, the fur of which is supposed to be superior to any that is known. The most valuable articles that we used in this traffic were hatchets, saws, old swords, large knives, and blue beads; but having very few of any of them left, we supplied the want of these with pewter plates, pieces of iron hoops, old buckles, buttons, etc., and, in fact, anything made of iron, tin, copper, or brass. The principal motive of our procuring those skins was for clothing to secure us against the cold, for of the bearskins we made greatcoats, and with the furs lined our jackets and made caps and gloves, from which we found great comfort; and indeed we had need, for we experienced very little from our provisions, which were only just sufficient to keep us alive.

One can hear the talk of the ward-room when this journal is read. They lament continually their departure from fair Tahiti. They have no word of praise for the people in these cold latitudes: "They are the most filthy set we ever met with." As for the women, "I don't remember that more than two or three of them came off to the ships; they were dressed nearly in the same manner as the men, and like them had the most dirty appearance imaginable: being far unlike the blooming beauties of the Tropics."

He says nothing at all about a very curious circumstance mentioned by Cook, which would have increased his disgust had he observed it, namely, that some of the people brought half-eaten and half-roasted human heads and hands and offered them for sale. There is probably some mistake, as in no part of North America were the people ever cannibals. Though they were so unattractive to these poor fellows, sick with longing for the delightful fruits and soft airs and blooming beauties of the tropics, they managed to afford a certain amount of amusement.

They used frequently as they lay alongside in their canoes to entertain us with their war songs and a very curious kind of masquerade dance, in which they put on large wooden masks of various forms and colours, and shifted them with great dexterity. The greater part of them resembled the face of a man; the features were cut out larger, but very expressive and well executed, and represented a number of droll gestures and distortions; they had hair eyebrows and teeth to them, and were painted very curiously; some of them were made to resemble the heads of wild beasts; and others that of a bird with the bill to open and shut at pleasure. The two latter ones they frequently made use of in hunting, by way of deception to decoy those animals near them that they are in search of.

The people and place occupy two long chapters very carefully put together in the history. It seems certain that Cook and Anderson, to both of whom we are indebted for these chapters, never communicated to the other officers the orderly and methodical system of research into manners and customs which they brought to their own work among the natives. In many respects the methods recommended by modern students of anthropology might have been based upon those followed by Cook and his sagacious assistant.

On leaving the Sound the ships proceeded northward along the shore. Here the history becomes little more than a log, showing the course, the discoveries of islands, inlets, rivers, and headlands. There is not a word in Cook's journal to show that the ship's provisions were anything but abundant. It is from Gilbert that we hear of short commons and grumbling. But it must be remembered that the captain fared no better than his officers or his men. "Here," says Gilbert, " a boat was sent on shore with a few people to haul the seine for fish. We caught several cod alongside with hook and line, which were a most welcome acquisition to us, being almost starved with hunger." A few days later there is another welcome acquisition. "Four or five small canoes came off to us with one or two men in each, and brought with them a few fresh salmon, which we purchased, and heartily wished for more: these serving only to raise our desires for what we could not procure, as they did not come off to us again." Happily, being becalmed off an island, they caught a great quantity of halibut, "afforded us an excellent feast for four or five days." In common gratitude they named the island after the fish, and for all I know the island still bears that name. In these seas there was a great deal of fog, and the shores were still covered with snow. On August 4th, "William Anderson, the surgeon and observer, died of consumption from which he had long been declining. Gilbert mentions the circumstance without any comment. The captain says of him: "He was a sensible young man, an agreeable companion, well skilled in his own profession, and had acquired considerable knowledge in other branches of science. The reader of this journal will have observed how useful an assistant I had found him in the course of the voyage; and had it pleased God to have spared his life, the public, I make no doubt, might have received from him such communications on various parts of the natural history of the several places we visited, as would have abundantly shown that he was not unworthy of this commendation."

It seems rather cold praise, but it is a true and faithful acknowledgment of duty, and as much as could be expected of a man who loved nothing but work, and saw no special merit in a man's working his best. As for the observations referred to, they are, as I have already explained, incorporated in the history by Bishop Douglas. Anderson's papers were all handed over to the Admiralty, but those which concerned natural history were given to Sir Joseph Banks. Poor Anderson was fated to receive scant praise. Banks could only say of him that had he lived he would have given to the world something that would have done him credit. This great mass of observation was incorporated with Cook's journal, is not that creditable to Anderson? One would have liked a little more about Anderson, who interests us above all the rest of the company which followed Cook. Gilbert might have told us that he was ill: he might at least have said a word as to the way in which his death was received; but that is not a sailor's way. When a man dies, the event is recorded, and the body dropped overboard, that is all; his place is filled up and nothing more is said. The cold and fogs met with in this part of the voyage clearly accelerated the end of Anderson; they proved trying to the whole crew, as is evident from Gilbert's journal. He gives us at this point an account of the sea-horse, which shows considerable powers of observation. The details concerning the preparation of the carcass for food are wanting in Cook's account. He says:

By seven o'clock in the evening we had received on board the *Resolution* nine of these animals, which, till now, we had supposed to be sea-cows, so that we were not a little disappointed, especially some of the seamen, who, for the novelty of the thing, had been feasting their eyes for some days past. Nor would they have been disappointed now, nor have known the difference, if we had not happened to have one or two on board who had been in Greenland, and declared what animals these were, and that no one ever ate of them. But notwithstanding this we lived upon them as long as they lasted, and there were few on board who did not prefer them to our salt meat.

Hear now Gilbert's account of these animals, and of the delectable food they afforded.

During this cold and disagreeable passage we met with great numbers of sea-horses, but why they are so called I can't imagine, for they bear not the smallest resemblance to that animal. They are about the size of a large ox, and have a thick hide thinly covered with short bristly hair; their heads are very small, and is the only part about them that has the least appearance to a beast, the rest of the body being like a fish, the hinder parts tapering and terminating in a couple of fins about two feet long instead of feet; having likewise one upon each shoulder, with which they swim faster than can be imagined, but more slowly upon the ice. They have two large white ivory teeth like those of the elephant projecting with a small curve downwards from their upper jaw; which are from one and a half to two feet in length and nearly parallel to each other at about five inches distance, and end in a point at the outer extremities. That they are endued with a greater share of sagacity and understanding than the generality of animals will appear from the following instance: when they went to sleep, a great number of them assembled upon a small piece of ice separated from the rest, and only just large enough for that purpose; that they may the more readily get off from it into the water in case of the approach of an enemy. I believe the only one they are apprehensive of is the white bear, which is likewise amphibious; and being much nimbler upon the ice then they are, has there greatly the advantage of them; but in the water the sea-horse is the swiftest and most formidable on account of its teeth. Therefore to prevent being surprised in their sleep they always appoint one as a sentinel and place it in the middle to keep watch over them during that time: which charge is strictly and faithfully performed, keeping the fore parts of its body erect, and an attentive eye all round; as we approached them with the ships they would lie very quiet till we came within two cables' length of them, when the one that had the watch would make a great noise to alarm the rest, upon which they all began by degrees to raise their heads and shoulders and look round them, and then crawl to the edge of the ice, and plunge head foremost into the water; so that by the time we had got within half a cable's length of them, there would not be one remaining. The noise they make is a mean betwixt the barking of a dog and the bellowing of an ox. We hoisted out our boats to get some, and with great difficulty killed and brought on board eight or ten of them; for although we rowed ever so softly, yet by the time we got within good musket shot, it was a great chance if there were any left; and unless we fired at them upon the ice it was twenty to one that we could hit them in the water, as they dive immediately. They will in general bear three or four balls in their bodies before they are killed, except in their heads, and then one is sufficient. Their affection for their young and even for one another is very great and remarkable, for wherever one of them got wounded in the water, if any of the rest were near, they would come to its assistance and carry it off if possible at the risk of their own lives; but if by chance we had killed one of their young, the mother would come and make every attempt to rescue it from us, and even try to upset the boat it was in, by hooking the boat side with her teeth, which she would follow till she was killed, all the time making a lamentable noise and showing every sign of real parental distress.

After we had got them on board they were skinned and cut up by the butcher; the hides we preserved for the rigging, the blubber or fat we put into casks to melt down into train oil for our lamps; and the flesh, disgustful as it was, we ate through extreme hunger, caused by the badness of our provisions and short allowance, which were but just enough to exist upon, and were now reduced on account of this supply; the quality of which will be best described in the several preparations it went through before it was possible to eat it.

In the first place, we let it hang up for one day that the blood might drain from it, which would continue to drop for four or five days, when permitted to remain so long, but that our hunger would not allow of at first; after that we towed it overboard for twelve hours, then boiled it four hours, and the next day cut it into steaks and fried it; and even then it was too rank both in smell and taste to make use of, except with plenty of pepper and salt, and these two articles were very scarce amongst us; however, our hunger got the better of the quality, and in the quantity we found some comfort, having as much of it as we could eat, which was what we had been a long time unaccustomed to; we salted some of it by way of experiment, which, after lying two or three weeks, we found was a little improved; but still could only be eaten by such as were at the point of perishing with hunger, and where no other food was to be secured.

The most northerly point reached was in lat. 69° 36'. They were then in the region of Polar ice. As there was but little wind the captain went out with the boats to examine the state of the ice and the manner of its formation. He arrived at the conclusion, since fully confirmed, that it is vain to expect that these seas are ever free from ice, or to believe that the sun of an Arctic summer is ever strong enough to melt the ice formed in the winter.

I am of opinion (he says) that the sun contributes very little towards reducing these great masses. For although that luminary is a considerable while above the horizon, it seldom shines out for more than a few hours at a time, and often is not seen for several days in succession. It is the wind, or rather the waves raised by the wind, that brings down the bulk of these enormous masses by grinding one piece against another, and by undermining and washing away those parts that lie exposed to the surge of the sea. This was evident from our observing that the upper surface of many pieces had been partly washed away, while the base or under-part remained firm for several fathoms round that which appeared above water, exactly like a shoal round an elevated rock. . . . Thus it may happen that more ice is destroyed in one stormy season than is formed by several winters, and an endless accumulation is prevented. But that there is always a remaining store, every one who has been upon the spot will conclude, and none but closet studying philosophers will dispute.

The journal here resumes the baldness of a log; the ship's course was southward again among the islands off Alaska. On one of them Cook remarks: "We found a heath abounding with a variety of berries." Gilbert as usual expresses the emotions of the crew at the *Discovery* of these berries.

This part of the coast, which is very mountainous inland, but toward the shore is of a moderate height and thinly covered with small pines; this being the first wood we had seen since we had left Cook's River, it was quite a new sight to us and appeared very delightful. "We found hurtle and crane berries here in great plenty, which proved a far more delicious treat to us than the fruits of the tropical islands; being at present in much greater want of them; yet we got but few, as we were allowed to go on shore only for a very short time. We took in some water here and a great quantity of wood, the beach being almost covered with old trees and branches that had drifted upon it. As we could not get any farther with the ships, two boats were sent well armed, under the command of Mr. King, our second lieutenant, to examine the head of the sound and discover if the land on the south side joined to this on the north. We saw about twelve of the natives, from whom we purchased several salmon trout, which were very acceptable to us. After three days we weighed and stood over to the other side of the sound, which is here about seven leagues across, and anchored within a bluff point that stretched a little way out and formed a small bay to the westward of it; we landed and found great plenty of berries and a few currant bushes, but they had no fruit left upon them. We gathered great quantities of an herb that grows here, to make use of in lieu of tea ; which has a very agreeable flavour, and is the same kind as is used by the Indians of Hudson's Bay and Newfoundland.

Among these islands and on the coast of Kamschatka they fell in with Russians, from whom they got such information as these settlers could give and the sight of their charts. It was not until the end of October that Cook finally left Oonalashka and steered south, appointing the Sandwich Islands as the place of rendezvous for the *Discovery*. During this voyage in the North Pacific twelve hundred leagues of coast were examined, and the sea traversed in many directions. No other navigator had ever before done so much for this part of the world. Yet the expedition failed in its main object and found no north-east passage.

On December 1st the *Resolution* reached the Sandwich Islands once more, and discovered the islands of Mowee (Maui) and Owhyhee (Hawaii). Gilbert again expresses for us the satisfaction of the crew upon arriving at a place of rest and refreshment after this long voyage.

The joy that we experienced on our arrival here is only to be conceived by ourselves, or people under like circumstances; for after suffering excess of hunger and a number of other hardships most severely felt by us for the space of near ten months, we had now come into a delightful climate, where we had almost everything we could wish for in great profusion; and this luxury was still heightened by our having been at a shorter allowance of provisions this last passage than ever we were at before. Having procured a sufficient supply to last us four or five days, we stood off and worked up along shore to the S.E., keeping at the distance of five or six leagues from the land; when our stock on board began to grow short, we went close in and traded for more, and then stood off again; this we continued to do for ten or twelve days, till we weathered the S.E. point of the island, which is called by the natives Mowwee.

We have now arrived at the last act in the life of Captain Cook. As regards the people who were to be his murderers, almost his last words express his confidence in the natives and his satisfaction with their conduct.

I had never met with a behaviour so free from reserve and suspicion, in my intercourse with any tribes of savages, as we experienced in the people of this island. ... It is to be observed to their honour that they never once attempted to cheat us in exchanges, nor to commit a theft. They understand trading as well as most people, and seemed to comprehend clearly the reason of our plying upon the coast. . . . We moored with stream-anchor and cable to the northward, unbent the sails, and struck yards and topmasts. The ships continued to be most crowded with natives and were surrounded by a multitude of canoes. I had nowhere in the course of my voyage seen so numerous a body of people assembled at one place. For besides those who had come off to us in canoes, all the shore was covered with spectators, and many hundreds were swimming round the ship like shoals of fish. We could not but be struck with the singularity of the scene; and perhaps there were few on board who ever lamented our having failed in our endeavours to find a northern passage homeward last summer. To this disappointment we owed our having it in our power to revisit the Sandwich Islands, and to enrich our voyage with a *Discovery* which, though the last, seemed in many respects to be the most important that had hitherto been made by Europeans throughout the extent of the Pacific Ocean.

These are the last written words of Captain Cook, if indeed he did write them, which only Bishop Douglas can tell us. It is singular not only that his confidence should prove so mistaken, but that he should also so greatly exaggerate the importance of this new discovery. What is Hawaii, what are all the Sandwich Islands together, compared with New Zealand and Australia?

CHAPTER XI

HIS DEATH

THE Pacific, which loved to kill those who wrested its secrets, was now to claim as a victim the great sailor who had fixed on the chart all the floating and uncertain islands seen by previous voyagers, and had found so many more himself. The story of his death is the most remarkable in the whole history of ocean disaster. It was imperfectly told, because imperfectly understood, by King, Samwell, and others who witnessed it. The real explanation of the tragedy has been obtained from the people of Hawaii themselves. It will be found in the *History of Hawaii*, by Manley Hopkins, Hawaiian Consul-General. Let us tell the true story, made possible by the traditions and recollections of the natives themselves. Mr. Hopkins states that in 1823, when Mr. Ellis, the missionary, visited the island, he found many still living who had been present at the murder, or who remembered its occurrence. I can corroborate this statement, because I was myself assured of the fact by Mr. Ellis himself somewhere about the year 1865. He not only informed me that he had conversed with men who had been present and had seen the thing done, but he also gave me certain particulars concerning the murder which I unfortunately neglected to note. To the best of my recollection, however, in Hopkins's book these particulars are all recorded. The tale is one which the biographer would leave untold if possible. But it cannot be neglected. Cook was killed, who had shown a power of conciliation with the natives granted to no other navigator in these seas, Why?

Those who first boarded Cook's ships returned with astonishing reports. The people on board had heads horned like the moon; they carried fires burning in their mouths; they ate the raw flesh of men, this was the red water-melon. If they wanted anything they took it out of their bodies; and they voyaged, as anybody could see, on islands with high trees. This was the report.

Now, a long time ago, there lived, on the island of Hawaii, Lono the swine-god. He was jealous of his wife and killed her. Driven to frenzy by the act, he went about boxing and wrestling every man whom he met, crying, "I am frantic with my great love." He instituted the athletic games known as the Mahakiki in honour of his wife's memory, and sailed away from the island for a foreign land. Ere he departed he prophesied, "I will return in after-times on an island bearing cocoa-nut trees, swine, and dogs." Who should these strangers be but Lono, the great god Lono, come back again with his companions, every one an immortal of the lesser kind?

When Cook returned after a year's absence he first anchored in the Bay of Wailuhu on the northern shore of Maui He arrived the day after a great battle, in which the King of Hawaii, who had invaded the adjacent island, was victorious. To the victors it seemed now absolutely certain that Lono himself, the god of victories, had come in person to add lustre to their triumph. The news quickly spread over all the islands of the group.

When the ships anchored in the Bay of Kealakeakua it was in the middle of a week of *tabu*. No ordinary avocations were to be followed, no canoe must put out to sea, no one must bathe, no one must be seen out of doors. There must be no light, no fire, no noise. Only the kings and priests, descendants of the gods, might move about as usual. It was at one of these awful periods that Cook arrived for the second time. He was received in silence profound. Yet so strong was the belief that he was none other than Lono himself that the *tabu* was instantly removed. Great numbers of people went on board, among them a high chief named Palu and an old priest, who paid divine honours to the captain, throwing a red cloth over his shoulders and pronouncing a long oration. How far the English understood what was meant does not appear. Probably they took these ceremonies as simple proofs of friendship. But what followed could hardly be interpreted to mean simple friendliness or even respect.

The people, in their anxiety to see the great god Lono, flocked by tens of thousands. There were three thousand canoes afloat on the bay at one time. When the captain went on shore, heralds announced his approach, and opened a way for him through the crowds. As he moved, the assemblage covered their faces, and those nearest to him prostrated themselves on the earth in the deepest humility. As soon as Lono had passed, the people sprang up erect and uncovered their faces. The evolution of prostration and erection was found at last so inconvenient, and to require so unwonted an agility, that the practical-minded people found that they could best meet the case by going permanently on their hands and feet; and so at last the procession changed its character, and 10,000 men and women were seen pursuing or flying from Captain Cook on all fours. (Hopkins's History of Hawaii, p. 98.)

This would be only ridiculous, but what followed was more serious. King, who tells the story with all the details, certainly did not understand the meaning and the importance of the ceremonies. It is important also to note that neither Samwell in his account of the murder, nor Gilbert, knew anything about this wonderful function. The chief Koah, chief and priest, led Cook, who was accompanied by King and by Bayley the astronomer, to a certain *morai*, or sacred place, formed by a square solid pile of stones, forty yards long, twenty broad, and fourteen high. The top was flat and paved, surrounded by a wooden rail, on which were fixed skulls of sacrificed captives. In the centre of this area stood a minor building of wood; on the side next the country were five poles, upwards of twenty feet high, supporting an irregular kind of scaffold; at the entrance were two wooden images; and beside the poles were twelve images ranged in a semicircle. They invited the captain to climb upon the scaffold, and there, having wrapped him in red cloth, they proceeded to offer him a hog, two priests performing a kind of service with antiphonal chants in honour of the god Lono. When the captain came down he was invited to prostrate himself and to kiss a certain idol; this he apparently did without scruple. He was then placed between two wooden images of other gods; his face and hands were anointed with chewed cocoa-nut; he drank *aeow* prepared by mastication, and ate pork also masticated. On another occasion he visited a second temple, where similar ceremonies were performed, and always afterwards whenever he landed a priest attended him. These ceremonies, according to King, "so far as related to the person of Captain Cook, approached to adoration."

Clearly King understood nothing of the real meaning of these ceremonies. But there are preserved at Hawaii, among the histories and traditions made in the early days when the people were first encouraged to write down their recollections and legends, certain documents which state positively, and leave no doubt, that the story told above is true; that Cook was taken for the god Lono, and that the priests paid him divine honours as Lono, and caused the people to bring him offerings, the collection of which became very speedily a grievous tax, of pigs, fruit, and cloth.

When the king came back from Maui he paid a grand visit of ceremony to the ships, bringing gifts. He threw over Lono's shoulders his own cloak, adorned his head with his own helmet, and placed in his hands a curious fan, the insignia of royalty.

What did Cook mean by accepting these honours? The gifts of the king might have been accepted as a proof of friendship; but the prostration, the litany, the sacrifice, the kissing of the idol, what could these things mean? It seems as if he must have known that worship was intended, adoration, of something godlike, even if the fable of the god Lono was unknown to him. Indeed, there is no indication of his knowing anything about Lono, who is called in King's journal Orono, and interpreted to mean a title of high honour. We must conclude that Cook's attitude showed a readiness to accept any honours, provided only that they assisted in victualling his ships and promoting the success of the expedition. If they chose to worship him, they might.

The sequel proved that he would have done better to repudiate these honours. Two or three unfortunate incidents occurred. One of the seamen died. He was an old man named William Watman, who had served as a marine for twenty -one years; after that he sailed with Cook on his second voyage, and though by the captain's interest he obtained admission into Greenwich Hospital, he could not remain there, but must needs follow his master on his third voyage. He was buried on shore, the captain reading the service. Perhaps it would have been better to have buried him in the sea, and thus to have avoided connecting death in the minds of the natives with these strangers.

Then there was the unfortunate business about the fence which surrounded the sanctuary. This fence, actually this sacred fence, was demanded for fuel; it was not refused, nothing could be refused to Lono, and it was taken on board the ship, with many idols attached to it or leaning against it. One cannot understand the story except that Cook, in some blundering way, conceived the idea of showing the people how powerless were their idols. What should we think if some Protestant, using a power which had fallen to him, should demand the stripping of the figures and pictures of a Roman Catholic cathedral? Then there was a quarrel about the carrying of a rudder which had been taken ashore for repairs. Stones were thrown about and sticks freely used.

Perhaps in consequence of these things, but probably because they were already tired of their enthusiasm and of the expense which it entailed, the people had begun to show signs of impatience.

I could never learn (King writes and this is very useful in showing how little they understood of the popular superstition) anything further than that they imagined we came from some country where provisions had failed, and that our visit to them was merely for the purpose of filling our bellies. Indeed the meagre appearance of some of our crew, the hearty appetites with which we sat down to the fresh provisions, and our great anxiety to purchase and carry off as much as we were able, led them naturally to such a conclusion. ... It was ridiculous enough to see them stroking the sides and patting the bellies of the sailors (who were certainly much improved in the sleekness of their looks during our short stay in the island), and telling them, partly by signs and partly by words, that it was time for them to go, but if they would come again the next bread-fruit season they should be better able to supply our wants. We had now been sixteen days in the bay, and if our enormous consumption of hogs and vegetables be considered, it need not be wondered that they should wish to see us leave.

They sailed on February 4th, 1779, no doubt to the joy and relief of the people. The great god Lono, gratifying as it always is to gaze upon a god, had proved expensive. It was hoped that a generation or two would pass before his return. He took from them a great farewell present of food and cloth, and in return gave them an exhibition of fireworks.

A week afterwards the ships came back. The *Resolution* had sprung her foremast in a gale. There were no signs of welcome. The king had gone away and left the island under *tabu*. The priests, however, consented to receive the damaged spar and sails and to place them with a small guard of marines under special *tabu*.

But the old power was gone; the people had either ceased to believe that Cook was Lono, or, which is more probable, were so familiar with the appearance of the god and his companions as to revere them no longer. Then the marines in guard of the gear under repair did a very dreadful thing, they persuaded some of the women to break the *tabu* and visit them; in their wrath the islanders burned down their house after they had gone. There was a quarrel again about getting water. Finally there was a more serious trouble about one of the *Discovery*'s cutters, which was stolen, No other than the chief Palu himself, who had been the first to welcome the return of the god, stole that cutter. Can we imagine that he or the other chiefs and priests believed any longer in the divinity of Cook and his companions? Such a thing as the loss of the boat was an occasion on which Cook always showed great determination. He went on shore himself, resolved to make an example. He would capture the king and take him on board his ship, there to stay till the cutter was restored.

This was on the morning of Sunday, February 14th. The native account of what followed is thus given by Hopkins.

Cook having come on shore and had an interview with Kalaniopuu, the two walked together towards the shore, Cook designing to take the king on board his ship and detain him there till the missing boat should be restored. The people seeing this, and having their suspicions already roused, thronged round and objected to the king's going further. His wife, too, entreated that he would not go on board the ships. Kalaniopuu hesitated. While he was standing in doubt a man came running from the other side of the bay crying, "It is war. The foreigners have fired at a canoe from one of their boats and killed a chief! "On hearing this the people became enraged and the chiefs were alarmed, fearing that Cook would put the king to death. Again his wife Kanona used her entreaties that he would not go on board, and the chiefs joined with her, the people in the meantime arming themselves with stones, clubs, and spears. The king sat down, and Captain Cook, who seemed agitated, began walking towards his boat. Whilst doing so a native attacked him with a spear. Cook turned and with his double-barrelled gun shot the man who struck him. Some of the people then threw stones at the Englishman, which being seen by his men in the boats, they fired on the natives. Cook endeavoured to stop the firing, but on account of the noise he was unable to do so. He then turned to speak to the people on shore, when some one stabbed him in the back with a *palloa* or dagger, and at the same time a spear was driven into his body. He fell into the water and spoke no more.

Samwell and King agree in the main with this account. In the fight the Englishmen appear to have behaved with great courage, especially Phillips and Roberts. There was one exception: the lieutenant commanding the launch drew his boat off the shore. Had he joined Roberts, Samwell thinks that the catastrophe might have been avoided. He said himself, in defence, that he mistook his orders. That he was not charged with cowardice is said to have been due to the weak health of Clerke, who shrank from a measure so extreme, and was physically unable to examine into the question.

Let us now give Gilbert's narrative, if only to show how the tale was told by those of the expedition who knew nothing of the god Lono or the adoration, and were not eye-witnesses of the murder.

From hence we stood over to a large island called Owyhee, that lies in sight of it to the S.W., which we made on the N.E. side; it is very mountainous inland, and the shores in general steep, but exceeding fertile. The natives came off to us in great numbers and behaved in a very friendly manner; we traded with them as usual till we had purchased provisions enough for five or six days; which we did in three or four hours, and might have got three times as much if we had chosen, for the greatest part of their canoes were obliged to return to the shore with what they had brought off to us. We then stood off about 5 or 6 leagues from the land, and worked up along shore to the S.E., keeping at that distance till our stock was expended; and then went in and traded for more, as we had done off the other island. As we were not yet in want of water Captain Cook preferred this method of passing the time to going into a harbour; as it was a great means of saving trade, of which he was very apprehensive we should not have as much as we might have occasion for. The *Discovery* having broken an arm off one of her bower anchors at the Island of Desolation, the armourers were employed, while we lay in Samganoda harbour, in working it up for that purpose, which was proportionably divided betwixt the two ships, and with several spare iron stores, principally belonging to the shallop, served us for trade during our stay among the islands.

After standing off and on for upwards of a month, and having coasted along near two-thirds of the island, we began to be in want of water; therefore the master with two boats well armed was sent inshore to look for a harbour, and very luckily found a small bay opposite to us, which was the first we had seen the least appearance of: but however, as this could not be perceived till we came within two miles of it, we very probably might have passed others of the same kind. The next morning (being about the 10th of January 1779) we stood in for it with a light breeze; and as we approached near the shore we were surrounded with upwards of 1000 canoes at the mean rate of six people in each; and so very anxious were they to see us, that those who had none swam off in great numbers, and remained alongside in the water, both men, women, and children, for four or five hours, without seeming tired; the decks both above and below were entirely covered with them; so that when we wanted to work the ships we could not come at the ropes without first driving the greatest part of them overboard; which they bore with the utmost cheerfulness and good nature, jumping from every part of her into the water, as fast as they could, appearing to be much diverted at it, and would come on board again when the business was over.

This bay is situated on the west side of the island, in latitude $19\frac{1}{2}°$ N. and longitude 204° E., and is called by the natives Carnacoah. It is small and open to the sea, which causes a great swell to set in, and a great surf breaking on the shore renders the landing rather difficult; the bottom of it is a high steep cliff, but the sides are low and level, with a town upon each, at least eight times as big as any we had seen before in the south sea. The country here is one entire plantation, as far as we could see from the ship, which is divided into squares by stones thrown together or hedges of sugarcane; we moored with the bowers in 10 fathom of water, gravel bottom, about two-thirds of a mile from the town on the north side, and one -third from a low sandy beach on the south side; near the bottom of the bay, which is the only one in it.

We got our observatories and tents on shore here, as usual, and pitched them upon a large oblong piece of ground, walled round with stones, two or three feet high, which was held sacred by the natives, who, notwithstanding their curiosity, so great was their superstition, that none but the chiefs dare venture to come upon it, so that our people were the less disturbed by them. The sail makers were sent on shore with the greatest part of our sails to repair, they being now very much worn; as was all our rigging, which we carefully overhauled here.

We were surrounded every day with a great number of canoes, and supplied by the natives with provisions in the most plentiful and hospitable manner imaginable. The king of the island, whose name was Terriaboo, and several other very powerful chiefs, frequently came on board to visit Captain Cook, who always received them with the greatest respect; they generally brought with them a large present of hogs, fowls, fruit, etc., for which in return he gave them at different times four or five small iron daggers, about two feet and a half long, in form of their own wooden, ones, and made by the armourer for that purpose, likewise such other trinkets as they were pleased with. What one was most in want of here was good water; that which there is being in standing pools, and very muddy and brackish, except some we got from a small spring in a well, at the foot of a rock close to the beach, which yielded very little; and though it was clear and much better than the other, yet was rendered brackish from its being so near the water side. We purchased not less than 10 or 12 puncheons of excellent salt here, which is principally made by the sun, and was the first we met with during the voyage; this proved a very welcome supply, as it enabled us to salt down pork for sea, which otherwise we could not have done, having used all we had on board for that purpose at Otaheite. One of our seamen died here, whom we interred on shore in one of their burying-places. Captain Cook read prayers over him in the usual manner; and the natives who were present on the occasion, according to their custom threw a couple of small pigs and some fruit into the grave, which were covered up with him. The latter part of the time we lay in Matavai Bay in Otaheite, and at Amsterdam, one of the Friendly Islands, being five weeks at each; we found supplies of all kinds began to grow scarce; but that was far from being the case here; for everything was as plentiful the last day as when we first came in. Having got everything off from the shore, in the evening about seven o'clock we perceived the house to be on fire that our sail makers had worked in, which we were in general of opinion they did on purpose through some superstitious notion they had among them.

It being now about the 4th of February and the season approaching, after a stay of near a month we sailed from the bay with an intention of going to the westward to those islands we had been at before, to take in a supply of yams for sea, as they had got none here, but in this we were unfortunately prevented; for after working up along shore to the northward a considerable distance against a very strong breeze, we discovered a spring in the head of our foremast right athwart from one cheek to the other, which obliged us to put back to Carriacoak Bay, to repair it; and having a fair wind for it, we got in next day and moored as before.

We immediately began to unrig the ship as far as was necessary, and having raised a pair of shears with two main topmasts, we got out the foremast, which was hauled up upon the beach to be repaired, and the carpenters of both ships were sent on shore for that purpose. The place our tents were pitched upon before being close to the beach, we set them up again on the same spot for the people who were at work upon the mast, and Mr. King, our lieutenant, was ordered to superintend this duty, with a guard of about eight marines for their protection. The observatories were likewise sent on shore with the astronomical instruments; and several of our sails to repair, having split them while we were out.

The natives did not appear to receive us this time with that friendship that they had done before; our quick return seemed to create a kind of jealousy amongst them with respect to our intentions; as fearing we should attempt to settle there and deprive them of part if not the whole of their country. This idea Captain Cook took every method to remove, by telling and showing them the reason that obliged us to come in again, with which they apparently seemed to be very well satisfied. The third day we had been here, in the afternoon, one of the natives on board the *Discovery* stole a pair of tongs from off the armourer's forge, and got into his canoe with them; the alarm being given, several of them began to paddle away as fast as they could; upon this the master, with a midshipman and two men, instantly got into their jollyboat, and without any arms pursued the canoe they suspected, which reached the shore long before them, and the men had got out and hauled it upon the beach, where several others were lying. The master and midshipman landed amongst a great number of the natives, and were going to seize one of the canoes, when a chief who was present told them that it belonged to him and they should not have it;

and indeed it is very probable but they mistook the one the man got into who committed the theft, either in putting off from the ship, among so many, or in hauling up; but as they still foolishly persisted in attempting to take it away, the chief laid hold of them and gave them a severe beating with his hands, which the two men who remained in the jollyboat perceiving, they rowed off to a little distance and got clear; our pinnace, that was lying not far off waiting for Captain Cook with only the crew in her, who seeing the affair, went without any orders to their assistance; but as soon as they came near the shore, the natives laid hold of the boat and hauled her up high and dry upon the beach, and broke some of the oars; which obliged the crew to take to the water and swim to the jollyboat, the Indians at the same time pelting them with stones. In a little time they were quiet, and called to the people in the boat to come on shore, and that they would let them have the pinnace; which they did, with the oars that remained, and likewise released the master and midshipman.

About an hour afterwards Captain Cook, hearing of the quarrel, was very angry, and gave our people a severe reprimand for their rashness; he walked round with one of the officers to the place where it happened, and found everything there very peaceable.

The next morning, which was the 14th February 1779, at daylight the *Discovery* found her six-oared cutter missing, that had been moored at the buoy, which we immediately supposed to have been stolen by the natives, in consequence of the above quarrel. When Captain Cook was informed of it, he ordered a boat from each ship, well armed, to row off the mouth of the bay to prevent the canoes from going out, and if any attempt it, to seize and send them in again; at the same time, proposed to Captain Clerke for him to go on shore and endeavour to persuade the king to come on board, that he might confine him till the boat was returned, according to his usual custom in these cases, but he seemed to express a desire to decline it on account of his health. Captain Cook said no more about the matter, but went himself with three boats, viz. a six-oared pinnace, in which he had with him a mate, the lieutenant of marines, and some of his men; a six-oared launch, with, the 3rd lieutenant, a mate, some marines, and a few additional seamen; and a four-oared cutter, with a mate and the midshipmen that rowed her; being in all, including the crews of the launch and pinnace, about 38 people, with each a musket, a cutlass, and cartridge-boxes. Having landed at the town on the north side of the bay with the lieutenant of marines, a sergeant, corporal, and seven private men, he ordered the boats with the rest of the people to lie off at a little distance, and wait for him. He then proceeded with the marines under arms up to the king's house, which was about two hundred yards from the water side; where he found him with several chiefs and not less than two or three thousand of the natives. After the usual ceremonies had passed, the captain invited him to come on board, which at first he absolutely refused, but after being pressed for some time he seemed inclinable to consent, and it was thought he would have come had he not been prevented by the chiefs, who would not permit him, as in all probability they saw into the design. This enraged Captain Cook very much, as he was not accustomed to have his intentions frustrated by any person, and had but little command over himself in his anger; at this instant a canoe came over from the other side of the bay, and brought the natives intelligence that a chief was killed there by one of our boats firing on shore; upon this they began to arm themselves with spears and pieces of the branches of trees that they broke up in a hurry instead of clubs; and some of the chiefs had the same iron daggers that we had given them; the Captain had with him a double-barrelled piece, one loaded with small shot, the other with ball, and a hanger by his side. They now began to press together and grew rather tumultuous, and some in particular insulting him, he beat them with the butt end of his musket, which caused them to be still more so; Mr. Philips, the lieutenant of marines, perceiving this, repeatedly told Captain Cook of the danger he apprehended they were in, and urged him to retire, which, as if Fate had determined he should fall, he took not the least notice of; but fired at one of them with small shot and wounded him, and a little afterwards at a chief with ball; but missing him killed the man that stood next to him outright, and although this enraged them to the highest degree, yet they then did not dare to attack him.

At last, finding it was impossible to accomplish his design, he ordered the marines to retreat, and was himself following them, and possibly would have got safe off, had not the people in the boats very unfortunately, on hearing the second report of his musket, begun to fire upon the natives, which threw them into a state of fury; the marines likewise on shore without orders followed their example; and Captain Cook had no sooner got to the water side and waved to the boats to give over firing, when one of the chiefs, more daring than the rest, stepped behind and stabbed him betwixt the shoulders with an iron dagger; another at that instant gave him a blow with a club on the head, by which he fell into the water; they immediately leaped in after and kept him under for a few minutes, then hauled him out upon the rocks and beat his head against them several times; so that there is no doubt but that he quickly expired. The marines likewise at the same time, after they had discharged their pieces, were closely attacked, and, not being able to load again, the corporal and three private men that could not swim were seized and killed upon the spot. The lieutenant, sergeant, and the other four leaped into the water, which was four or five feet deep close to the rocks, and escaped to the pinnace, which was lying within thirty yards of the shore; but by reason of the continual showers of stones that were thrown at them and the confusion of those people getting in, they could not afford the least assistance to Captain Cook, and very narrowly escaped from being taken. The launch, that lay close without her, and the cutter, that was inshore at a little distance, both kept up a brisk fire for the space of ten or fifteen minutes till they were obliged to retire; having killed and wounded several of the natives, and caused the greatest part of them to retreat; and we were informed by the gentlemen in the cutter, who were the last that left the shore, that very few of them remained by the dead bodies when the launch and pinnace came away. During the firing on shore we saw a great number of the natives running away up an adjacent hill, at whom we fired five or six shot from our great guns, but our first lieutenant would not allow of any more.

When on the return of the boats informing us of the Captain's death, a general silence ensued throughout the ship for the space of near half an hour; it appearing to us somewhat like a dream that we could not reconcile ourselves to for some time. Grief was visible in every countenance; some expressing it by tears, and others by a kind of gloomy dejection, more easy to be conceived then described: for as all our hopes centred in him our loss became irreparable, and the sense of it was so deeply impressed upon our minds as not to be forgot.

Such was the confusion of the people when they came on board that they did not perceive till a quarter of an hour afterwards how many of the marines were missing; Mr. Philips, the lieutenant, who behaved with great prudence and courage, received a large wound upon his shoulder by a spear, and one of the private men was wounded in his cheek close below his eye, two inches and a half of the point of a spear having broken short off and was buried in his head; the others had several bruises from the stones that were thrown at them, but suffered no hurt of any consequence. During this, our people on the south side of the bay, under the direction of Mr. King, the second lieutenant, were very fortunately reinforced by some of our boat's crew that had been rowing off the mouth of the bay before any disturbance had begun there; being then altogether about twenty-four in number, though not above two-thirds of them had muskets, on perceiving they were likely to be attacked they took possession of a burying place that lay near them; which was a large platform of earth thrown up and fenced with stones, being about a hundred and fifty yards in length, sixty in breadth, and the sides six or eight feet perpendicular all round, except a small passage, where not more than two people could go up abreast. Nothing could be more conveniently situated than this place; as from thence they could not only protect the masts, tents, and observatories, which lay between them and the beach and within less than a musket shot, but were secure from an encounter that they would not have been able to resist. The natives did not venture either to make an open effort to force them from their post or to come near the tents, but kept up a distant and vigorous attack by heaving a great number of stones from behind the trees and houses which lay behind them. By creeping along under cover of these walls, they were able to approach very close to the platform without being seen; and when they thought themselves near enough would stand up and heave several stones, and then retire for more; this they continued for some time, and when any of them fell, another of them would step forth and carry off the body at the risk of his own life. These Indians use a large thick mat, which they hold before them by way of a shield against their own wooden spears; and at the beginning of the attack several of them came to the edge of a pool, within reach of the shot, to dip them in the water, and then would hold them up in defiance, thinking by that means to quench the fire of the musket by which they supposed they were killed; but in that point we quickly undeceived them. The *Discovery*, lying nearest over to this side, fired several shot on shore, which terrified them very much.

After two or three hours they retired with the loss of six or eight killed and some wounded, finding it vain to carry on anything further against our people in their present situation, and thinking, I suppose, by that means to draw them from it; but they wisely kept possession of their post.

About two hours after the death of Captain Cook we went with all the boats from both ships well manned and armed, and brought them off, with the mast and everything else we had on shore very safe, the natives not daring to molest us. The remainder of the forenoon we were employed in getting the mast upon the booms for the carpenters to work at; they having done very little to it as yet.

Captain Clerke now came on board, and took the command of the *Resolution*, and appointed Mr. Gore, our first lieutenant, to that of the *Discovery*, and Mr. Harvey, one of the mates, to be lieutenant in his room.

In the afternoon, notwithstanding what had passed, two of the natives from the town on the north side of the bay had courage to come alongside, which was placing great confidence in us, and proves the high opinion they entertain of our integrity. One of them was a priest, whom we had often before known to have behaved very treacherously, therefore supposed in the present case that he had no good intentions towards us; and so highly were our people exasperated at the sight, that it was with great difficulty the officers could prevent their firing at him. After staying about a quarter of an hour he returned to the shore, and continued to make these short visits on board every forenoon and afternoon, for three or four days afterwards; which I believe was to see whether or not we were making any further preparations against them. Mr. King, now our first lieutenant, was sent off to the town on the north side with all our boats well manned and armed to treat with the natives for the bodies; carrying a white flag as a signal of peace for that purpose. They were assembled along the shore in great numbers, with their weapons in their hands and bidding us defiance in the most contemptuous manner imaginable; for they seemed to pride themselves very much in having killed our principal chief. But from what we afterwards learnt they had very little reason, having lost not less than eight or ten chiefs and about twenty common men, besides several wounded; amongst whom chanced to be the greatest part of those who assisted in the murder of our people. They strove much to persuade us to land, but without effect. One of them was dressed in Captain Cook's jacket and trousers, and another had his hanger in his hand, which he kept shaking at us, and making use of every threatening and insolent gesture he could possibly invent. This enraged the sailors to the highest degree, and it was with the utmost difficulty they were restrained from firing upon them. Finding we would not come any nearer, two of them ventured to swim off to us; whom we informed that we had no intentions of making an attack, but came only to demand the bodies, which, to amuse us for the present, they said were carried away some distance into the country; that we could not have them then, but promised to bring them off to us in the morning; therefore perceiving they were not to be procured at that time, the boats returned on board.

We were rather apprehensive that they intended to make an attack upon the ships in the night; therefore took every necessary precaution to prevent being surprised, by keeping our guns and swivels loaded, and sentry forward, abaft, and on each gangway, one-third of the people always under arms, and a four-oared cutter well armed constantly rowing round us, at a little distance, while it was dark; which both ships continued to do during our stay here.

The next morning the seamen earnestly solicited the captain that they might go on shore with their arms to revenge the death of their old commander, which he did not think proper to permit; as it was not the intention of the officers to pursue measures of that kind for a quarrel we had principally brought upon ourselves; but perceiving they were very eagerly bent upon it, he framed an excuse to pacify them for the present, by telling them he could not possibly think of allowing it whilst the ships remained in such a defenceless state, but that in two days' time, when we had got things into a little order, they should have leave for that purpose. By keeping them thus in suspense for three or four days their rage began to abate; and it is well he did, for had he at first positively denied them, so highly were they incensed against the natives, that I believe the officers would not have been able to have kept them on board. Being rather suspicious that they were assembling canoes round the north point of the bay, a boat with an officer was sent to see, who found no appearances of any. The forenoon a canoe with three men in her came off from the north side about half-way to the ship, where they stopped and began to throw stones towards us; in which they could not heave half that distance, they could not have any other intention but that of insulting of us: one of them all the time very triumphantly kept waving Captain Cook's hat over his head, till some muskets were fired at them, and then they instantly put back to the shore.

Our chief object at present was the foremast, which the carpenters of both ships were working upon with the utmost expedition, making new cheeks for it out of a spare anchor stock. In the afternoon, seeing a great number of the natives assemble upon the shore on the north side of the bay, we fired a few shot at them from our great guns, which quickly dispersed them.

When the old priest came on board we inquired of him concerning the bodies, but could get no satisfactory account of them; and when we asked him why they were not brought off, agreeable to the promise made yesterday, he said that they had been carried to different parts of the island, and were not yet collected together, but that we should have them the next day; which we perceived was only an excuse to keep us quiet, therefore gave over every hope of having them returned, as judging that they had otherwise disposed of them, and did not wish us to know in what manner. On the 16th nothing remarkable happened till about nine o'clock in the evening, when some people were discovered paddling very softly to the ships. It being quite dark, and (knowing?) not knowing how many there might be, two or three of the sentries instantly fired at them; nevertheless they persisted coming towards us, and finding there was only one small canoe, we suffered her to come alongside; when to our great astonishment they proved to be two of the natives, who had brought with them about five pounds of human flesh, which they told us was Captain Cook's, and that they were sent by a priest that lived on the south side of the bay, who had before always treated us with great hospitality; we learnt that he and his adherents still remained firmly attached to us, but were too few to declare it to their countrymen, which was the reason of their coming in the dark, that it might not be known. After giving them some presents, they returned to the shore, having luckily escaped being hurt in approaching the ship. This small remains of our unfortunate commander, which appeared to have been taken from the inside of his thigh, was all our friend could procure for us, and a great proof of his sincerity; but answered no good purpose to us, as the sight of it struck every one with horror, and tended only to disquiet the sailors, by renewing their desire to be revenged of the natives, which began to wear off.

Beginning now to be greatly in want of water, we were necessitated to go on shore again at all events, and endeavour to get off a sufficiency to last us to some other place; accordingly in the morning of the 17th we sent the two launches full of casks to a small well, before mentioned, on the south side close above the beach, with other boats, manned and armed, to protect them. The *Discovery* also hauled close in for that purpose. We had not been long ashore before the natives began to annoy us by throwing stones from behind the houses; and the well being situated at the foot of a steep hill they kept rolling large ones down from the top of it, which were often near doing us much mischief. To prevent this, in a great measure, it was determined by the

officers to set fire to the adjacent houses, which would not only terrify them, but hinder their approaching to molest us; as they then would have no shelter from our muskets. Therefore, when the people went on shore again after dinner, several of them were given port fires for that purpose; when it was amazing with what alacrity they carried this scheme into execution, the eagerness with which they grasped at this small opportunity of revenge being so great, that the officers could not keep them in the least order, for they all instantly separated and were guided only by their own impetuosity, setting fire to the houses, and killing the natives wherever they met with any, who were struck with such terror at seeing the flames that they made off as fast as they could; and it was very fortunate that they did, for our people were so much scattered, that had they made the least resistance, they might have cut several of them off, and the rest of us known nothing of it, till this business was over, which was in about an hour, when with great difficulty we collected the people together, and stopped their further progress: during this they had burnt about thirty houses, and killed six of the natives. Two Irishmen concerned in the affair extended their malice even to the dead bodies, by cutting the heads from two of them, which they brought down and fixed upon the stems of the boats. While the houses were yet blazing we perceived a party of them coming down the hill, but upon some of our people firing a few muskets at them they immediately fell flat on the ground and lay still for about five minutes; they then got up, and advanced slowly towards us with white flags in their hands, and finding they were not very numerous, we suffered them to approach us; when they proved to be our friend the priest, whom I mentioned last, with some of his followers, coming to entreat for peace for himself and his people. His house, being unknown to us, was unfortunately burnt with the others: we carried him on board the ships, where we consoled him in the best manner we could, and made him several presents, being well convinced of his sincerity to us. When the natives that came down the hill perceived the two bodies lying without their heads, they set up a most frightful cry, followed with great lamentation, seemed to be more affected at that than anything we had done to them, which must arise entirely from superstition.

I cannot proceed without mentioning an instance of remarkable courage in one of these Indians, who had for some time greatly annoyed the waterers by throwing stones at them from behind the rocks. At last, being closely pursued by several of our people, he retreated to a deep narrow cave, and immediately began raising a small breastwork of stones towards the bottom of it, behind which he placed himself; they searched all round, but to no purpose; and it is a doubt whether they would have found him or not, had not he discovered himself by throwing stones at them the instant they appeared. Upon this three or four of them stepped to the entrance of the cave and presented their muskets at him, and at the same time made signs, and told him that if he would come out he should not be hurt; when, like Æneas, he returned an answer with a flying stone, which was followed by others as fast as he could throw them. They then fired at him five or six times, at which he seemed to be not in the least intimidated, still persisting in throwing at them; but perceiving that he was much wounded and resolved to fight to the last moment, one of them rushed in upon him, clapped a pistol to his breast, and instantly despatched him; on examining him we found he had received no less than four balls, in different parts. He was a tall, well-made, handsome young man, and had the appearance of a chief. We took one of the natives prisoners that was attempting to escape in his canoe, whom we bound hand and foot and put him into a boat that had the head of one of his countrymen on the stem of it. In the evening the boat returned on board, having got a sufficiency of water to last us to Towi, one of the other islands where we knew we could get plenty. The officers would not permit the seamen to bring the two heads into the ship, but obliged them to throw them into the water alongside.

The prisoner being brought upon the quarter-deck, and set down bound as before, everybody thronged round him, as is usual in such cases, when it is scarce possible to conceive how strongly every sign of fear was imprinted in his countenance; he was seized with a most violent trembling from head to foot; his complexion, which was naturally of a light copper, was changed to that of a pale lead colour; and he remained silent and immovable. His apprehensions of death in every horrid form appeared to be so strong as not to admit of the least ray of hope to his relief, and entirely deprived him of the faculty of speech. By his looks, which expressed the most exquisite distress, he seemed to implore for mercy, in a manner so affecting that it excited pity in every breast, and all being desirous for it we unbound him. He now thought we were going to put into execution what his fears had suggested; and when we returned him his canoe and told him that he might go on shore, he paid no attention to it for some time, imagining we did it only to insult him in his misery, by tantalising him with what he had too great a dread upon his mind to believe; but when he found we were in earnest, his excess of joy was then as predominant as his fears had been before, and his gratitude, which he expressed in the sincerest manner, was not disguised under the veil of politeness, but flowed from the heart free and uncorrupted. He had not been long on shore before he came off again, with his canoe loaded with whatever he could procure as a present to us; for which in return we gave him something of equal value; this he continued to do two or three times a day, and became a most faithful friend.

On the 19th the carpenter having finished the mast, after great difficulty it was got in; the hawser we had reeved for that purpose being so rotten that it stranded in five or six places as we were heaving, and we had no better on board. On the 20th, in the morning, a chief that we had not seen before came on board, to negotiate a peace with us; and promised to restore part of the captain's body. Accordingly in the afternoon Captain Clerke, with three or four boats well armed, went close inshore on the south side, where he concluded a peace with that chief, and brought on board Captain Cook's head and hands, which were all the remains we could possibly procure. The head was too much disfigured to be known, but one of the hands we were well assured was his, from a wound he had formerly received in it which made it remarkable. One of the natives brought about a handful of small human bones which he said belonged to the marines, whom they had burnt; we made several inquiries to know if they ate them, but could not find the least reason to believe so: for they seemed to express as great an abhorrence of such an act as any European. They told us that no part of Captain Cook was burnt, but what became of the remainder of his body we could not learn; they also brought off the double-barrelled piece he had with him when he was killed, but they had entirely spoiled it by beating the barrels quite flat at the muzzle. We could never get the least intelligence of the cutter that was stolen, which was the first cause of this unfortunate affair.

On the 21st some of the natives from the south side of the bay brought off provisions and began to trade with us as usual; but excepting the old priest, we were seldom visited by any of those on the north side, who did not seem so much inclined as the others to come to a reconciliation: yet from every appearance I make no doubt, had we remained there, but that in three or four weeks we should have been nearly upon as friendly terms with them as we were at our first coming.

In the afternoon we buried the remains of our much-lamented commander alongside, with every ceremony due to his rank; whose name will be perpetuated to after-ages and ever stand foremost on the list of British navigators.

On the 22nd, the ship being rigged again and ready for sea, in the morning we sailed out of the bay; having no desire to stay any longer at a place where we had suffered so great a misfortune.

Thus ended, ingloriously, and as the result of an ill-advised attempt at high-handed justice, the life of the greatest navigator of any age. I think there can be no doubt that the attack on Cook was rendered possible by a strong revulsion of feeling as regards his real character: king, priests, and chiefs were perhaps by this time ashamed of their own credulity, though certainly still afraid of the captain and his men. That they showed human passions and emotion, ate fiercely, drank freely, and made love, would by no means detract from their divinity. Quite the contrary. The god of the islanders was as much a god of animal parts and passions as the god of many people much more highly civilised. Neither king nor priest contemplated the murder of Cook; but among such people a quarrel soon leads to a fight, and in a fight somebody naturally gets killed. On the other hand, one does not know, perhaps it may have occurred to some native humorist, such things have been done to wonder how a god would look and behave with a spear stuck right through him.

Cook was dead.

In this journey he explored the unknown part of the North American coast from lat. 43° N. to lat. 70° N., that is to say, for 3500 miles. He proved the proximity of the continents of Asia and America; passed the straits between them and surveyed the coast on each side to such a height of northern latitude as to demonstrate the impracticability of a passage in that hemisphere from the Atlantic into the Pacific Ocean either by an eastern or a western course. In short, if we except the Sea of Amoor and the Japanese Archipelago, which still remain imperfectly known to Europeans, he has completed the hydrography of the habitable globe.

King's Journal. He may be forgiven a little exaggeration. Cook was not the first sailor in those seas, nor did he discover the straits, and the impossibility of a north-west passage was not quite proved.

CHAPTER XII

THE END OF THE VOYAGE

WHEN such of the remains of their captain as could be recovered had been buried, it was alongside and not on shore, with "every ceremony due to his rank," Captain Clerke put out to sea and the voyage was resumed. The remaining history of the expedition, told admirably by Captain King, seems like the last act of a play whose hero has disappeared. Briefly, they spent the summer off the coasts of Kamschatka, and in October steered a course for home by way of Japan, Macao, and the Narrow Seas. In August, Captain Clerke died of consumption after a long and languishing illness. He was succeeded by Captain Gore, and Lieutenant King was appointed to the *Discovery*. Gilbert was transferred to the *Resolution* with King, he does not say in what capacity.

On arriving off Macao all the gentlemen were ordered to hand over their journals, charts, drawings, and observations of all kinds taken during the voyage, and a diligent search was made amongst the sailors for anything they had jotted down. This was by order of the Admiralty, and in order to prevent the scramble for publication which experience had even then shown to follow after every such expedition. If the Admiralty had possession of everything written and noted by their officers, nothing except in general terms could be published; while, the drawings and observations of all kinds being reserved, no scientific value whatever could attach to vague narrative. One is here faced by a certain uneasiness respecting the journal from which so much has been taken. It is certainly written from copious notes, and it was certainly written after the voyage, because the author in more than one place shows that he is arranging his notes, and reserving certain remarks for a second visit to the place which he is partly describing. Did Mr. Gilbert then give up everything, as the Admiralty ordered? Or, which is certainly possible did the Admiralty return him, and other officers, their journals after the official publication? It matters very little, but the question insists on being put.

On reaching the Channel they met with winds so contrary that Captain Gore took the ships along the west coast of Ireland, and anchored at Stromness in the Orkneys. Here he sent Captain King to London with all the papers and reports, and after being detained a month at Orkney was able to sail for London. It is melancholy to remark that on this, the very last bit of the voyage, two more of the *Resolution* men died. On October 7th, 1780, "we lashed along the Sheer-hulk at Woolwich."

Thus ended this voyage, long and eventful, which failed in its primary object, yet succeeded in so many others. The passage from ocean to ocean was not to be discovered for eighty years to come. When it was discovered it proved to be useless. The world for three hundred years had been looking for a thing which was there all the time and could be put to no practical purpose. It is the history of a good many human enterprises. We seek St. Brandan's Island, we look for *Terra Australis Incognita*; and we find New Zealand and Cape Horn, the Continent of Australia, and the great Pacific Ocean, studded with islands as the firmament is studded by the stars.

CHAPTER XIII

THE SHIP'S COMPANY

WE can learn more about the individual officers and men belonging to Cook's three expeditions than would be expected by reading the journals of the voyages. Cook himself tells us nothing of his officers except in connection with special service, when he is always ready to give them credit. There are no private letters preserved, for the simple reason that it is no use writing letters when there is no post. We cannot ascertain the grumblings of the forecastle, or the criticisms of the wardroom, but something may be recovered from the journals themselves; and there was, as we have seen, the narrative of George Forster and the journal of Gilbert. Also there are the books of Ellis, Sydney Parkinson the draughtsman brought by Banks, and one or two more, from reading which one acquires some knowledge of the officers.

In general terms Cook makes known his solicitude for the welfare of his crew; he tells us how, directly they got into cold weather, he had the sleeves of their jackets lengthened with baize and gave them caps made of the same warm material; he dilates on the grand antiscorbutic effects of his malt, his sauerkraut, and his portable broth; he prides himself on his preservation of the crew from scurvy. We have seen how he made a kind of tea for the men from the leaves and twigs of the spruce; how he had celery and scurvy grass boiled in the peas and wheat, though the men at first would not eat them; how he made beer out of the sugar-cane, and when the men refused it knocked off their grog. We see how he sends out the young gentlemen on shooting parties, and allows them to accompany the scientific men on their botanical expeditions. We cannot but remark how careful he is to mention any officer who does any special service; and when he loses his surgeon, William Anderson, it is not a formal entry in the log that records his death, but a careful tribute to his worth and his attainments that shows his justice and his desire to give to every man the credit due to his zeal and knowledge.

But when the ship's beef is so rank that it can no longer be eaten even by the strongest stomach, when the biscuit is half eaten and wholly defiled by the cockroaches, when the crew is weakened by privation and bad food, when half the ship's company are down through having eaten poisonous fish, the captain says nothing. These things were part and parcel of such a voyage; those who cannot endure them had better not come a-sailing on the broad Pacific; sufficient happiness for them to escape the dreadful scurvy and to come home again, at length, alive. Once or twice, it is true, he mentioned things which have reached a pass beyond any previous experience. We learn, for instance, on one occasion how the ship was pestered with cockroaches, whose numbers could not be kept down. They swarmed everywhere; at night they made everything in the cabins seem to be moving about by their multitudes. They devoured the ink on labels and letters; they even climbed up into the rigging, and when the sails were unfurled they fell in thousands on the deck. The surgeon, Mr. Anderson, discovered that there were two kinds, the *Blatta Germanica*, a daylight companion, and the *Blatta Orientalis*, their joy by night. But this *Discovery* brought no comfort to the crew, as it could not help to get rid of them; and the cockroaches, although named and classified, went on multiplying.

Again, certain fish, the captain says, which were eaten by the officers and the petty officers caused a violent pain in the head and bones, with a scorching heat of the skin and a numbness in the joints. "It was a week or ten days before all the gentlemen recovered." Forster's account of the same misfortune shows what a narrow escape they all had of being poisoned.

Our ship now resembled an hospital. The poisoned patients were still in a deplorable situation; they continued to have gripes and acute pains in all their bones. In the daytime they were in a manner giddy, and felt a great heaviness in their heads. At night, as soon as they were warm in bed, their pains redoubled and robbed them actually of sleep. The skin peeled off from the whole body, and pimples appeared on their hands. Those who were less affected with pains were much weaker in proportion, and crawled about the decks emaciated to mere shadows. We had not one lieutenant able to do duty; and as one of the mates and several of the midshipmen were likewise ill, the watches were commanded by the gunner and the other mates.

One would think that so severe a visitation would have called for more than a mere note of passing sickness.

It may be judged from Forster's journal with how much heart the people, including even the scientific men on board, endured these privations and suffered this hardness. We can see the captain, his face set southwards, looking over the heads of the hungry and discontented crew. He is thinking how he can break through the wall of ice and learn what is beyond. They are wondering how long it will be before the captain will give up this foolishness and turn back to warmer climates. The officers and passengers shared, as Forster plainly tells us, in the general dejection. Their store of special provisions had long since vanished, and they were now reduced to the fare of the common sailors. "The hope of meeting with new lands had vanished; the topics of common conversation were exhausted; the cruise to the south could not present anything new, but appeared in all its chilling horrors before us." The conversation and opinions of Columbus's crew have only partly been preserved; but such as they were, such were those of Cook's officers and scientific passengers. They were ready to exchange all their chances of glory in the discovery of the *Terra Australis Incognita* for another month at Otaheite, among the fruits and the "blooming beauties" of that island. Many other instances will be found by him who reads not only the Voyages themselves, but also the books which belong to them and surround them, as the big fish is attended by the little fish. Always it is the same thing. The captain endures and murmurs not, the men endure and grumble.

As one makes his way through these volumes, a personal interest, as I have already said, is presently awakened in the officers. Some of them begin to stand out clear of outline; we see their faces, we hear their voices.

Among these is Captain Clerke, he who follows at Cook's heels in the *Discovery*. He is a silent shade and pensive; he carries out instructions and endures hardships, uncomplaining even though, perhaps, because, the hand of death is upon him. When his chief is killed he is carried, already in the last stage of consumption, on board the *Resolution*, to die in a few more weeks. Another, who stands out a clear and well-defined figure, is that of Anderson, the surgeon, who picked up the language everywhere, compiled the vocabularies, and wrote these admirable reports on the manners and customs of the people, one of the earliest and best of anthropologists, next to the captain the man most zealous and eager for the success of the expedition. He died before his chief. Then comes King, who wrote the conclusion of the journal, King, whom the natives loved and called Tinnee, a man of genial and winning manners, a favourite with all. He came home in command of the *Discovery*. They made him a post-captain, but four years after his return he died in the south of France. Then there is Gore, who succeeded Clerke in the command; we see a good deal of Gore; he is always going off with boats, sounding, surveying, examining, a capable officer; but apparently, since King wrote the journals, not gifted with the pen of the ready writer. He died in 1790, one of the Captains of Greenwich Hospital. There are also those stout fellows, Roberts, the first lieutenant; Phillips, who behaved with so much pluck at the murder of the captain; Samwell, the surgeon; Edgecumbe, the marine. There are the two Forsters, grumbling and discontented; the amiable youth Sydney Parkinson, draughtsman, who died; Monkhouse, the surgeon, who died; Charles Green, the astronomer, who died; Sparrman, the naturalist, whom we remember emerging from the bush where the natives had stripped him of everything but his spectacles.

As for Gilbert, from whose log I have quoted, he is a voice and nothing more. He was transferred from one ship to the other. On his return home he was promoted with the rest, but, as I have said already, he died shortly afterwards of smallpox.

I have mentioned Isaac Smith, the boy whom Cook took with him, his wife's cousin, midshipman on his first and mate on his second voyage. After his second voyage he was made lieutenant, and continued in active service till the year 1794, when his health gave way, and he retired, receiving the rank of admiral in the year 1804. He was the first Englishman who landed in Australia. When the captain went ashore he took the boy with him. "Now then, Isaac," he said, "you go first." And the lad jumped ashore. Admiral Smith after his retirement lived with his cousin the widow.

There are one or two of the crew who deserve mention. The old and faithful Watman, who followed Cook on the third voyage, never weary of the sea, has been already mentioned. It was an ill service that he did his master in dying at the juncture when the natives were trying to believe the strangers to be all gods and superior to death. Next, there is Corporal Lediard, that gallant marine who, next to Anderson, developed the greatest quickness in learning the language wherever they touched. He was by birth an American, and in the year 1786 he formed the project of walking across the continent of America. For that purpose he thought he would journey through Europe and across Siberia to Kamschatka, where their Russian friends of their last visit would perhaps take him across the straits. Sir Joseph Banks and others raised a sum of fifty pounds for him. With this slender provision he sailed to Hamburg, and thence to Copenhagen and Stockholm. He thought to find the Gulf of Bothnia frozen over; as it was not, he walked all round it, through Tornea to St. Petersburg. Here he found a convoy of military stores about to start for the use of one Billings, who had been on one of Cook's expeditions and had now taken service with the Russians, being employed in making surveys for the Russian Government on the north-west coast of America. He obtained permission to join this convoy, and in August reached the town of Irkutsk in Siberia. Thence he proceeded to Yakutsk, where he met with Captain Billings. He returned to Irkutsk, intending to pass the winter there. But in January he was arrested, brought back under the guard of an officer and two soldiers in a post-sledge for Moscow. He was then taken to the frontier and dismissed, with the Empress's prohibition ever again to set foot within her territories. What harm this poor soldier-sailor could possibly do to the empire of Russia is not apparent. Sir Joseph Banks heard from him from Konigsberg. He died in 1790, and his adventurous life has been written and may be read.

One feels a certain sympathy, too, with the Irishman who had been in the Danish service, and somehow seemed to have no country left, so that when he ran away with the intention of remaining away for the rest of his life, a general compunction was felt for him, and though he was brought back his punishment was no more than a fortnight in irons. Many tried to run away; a sailor in New Zealand, enticed from his duty by a girl; a midshipman and a sailor in Otaheite, thinking that life on such an island was better far than to go on ploughing the barren wave; they were caught, too, but not severely punished Cook was hard, but he could feel for those weaknesses of human nature which did not interfere with the proper discharge of work. Lastly, two men ran away with the six-oared gig, but this was off Macao. They were never heard of again. One pictures the reception which these misguided and unhappy sailors would meet with from the Chinese mariners who should chance upon them and their six-oared gig. One more reminiscence of the voyages. It is Christmas Day, the ship is in lat. 65° S. It is midsummer, so that the nights are short; but the skies and seas are hidden with continual fog, so that nothing can be seen around or above; the vessel is in the midst of ice, a wall of ice is before them, broken ice, floating ice, ice in small lumps and in great hills all about them. For months the crew have been saving up their brandy in readiness for this sacred day, which they keep by all getting drunk very drunk, says the historian, though the captain passes over the occurrence.

On the discipline of the ship a good deal might be said, but Cook must not be judged by the practice of modern days. The sailors get drunk unrebuked on Christmas Day, that would not be permitted in these days. When the ship was in port, things were allowed to go on aboard which can hardly now be related, they may be found in great detail in

Forster's book. At sea a stern rule prevailed, and the lash was freely used; on shore and in port the men did what they pleased. Those who know who went down on board the *Royal George* with brave Kempenfeldt will understand that Cook followed the usual practice. "Certain things," he said, "I permitted, because I could not prevent them." There might have been, one feels, some restrictions, an attempt at restraint, but there were none. It was exactly the same with Wallis.

One more point of difference. I know not when every ship began to carry its chaplain, but there was no chaplain on any of Cook's voyages. It was, however, the custom for the captain to read the service to the whole crew on Sunday mornings. The Bible from which Cook read the lessons during his last voyages was given to his widow, who used no other during the rest of her long life. It is a well-bound quarto,

Ed. Baskett, Oxford, 1765, and is now in Sydney with other relics of the great navigator.

CHAPTER XIV

THE LAST

IT seems idle to add anything concerning the character of James Cook to what has gone before. He was hard to endure, true to carry out his mission, perfectly loyal and single-minded, he was fearless, he was hot-tempered and impatient, he was self-reliant, he asked none of his subordinates for help or for advice, he was temperate, strong, and of simple tastes, he was born to a hard life, and he never murmured however hard things proved. And, like all men born to be great, when he began to rise, with each step he assumed, as if it belonged to him, the dignity of his new rank. A plain man, those who knew him say, but of good manners. If this volume does not show the manner of the man, then it has failed. Such as his achievements required, such he was.

Let us, however, once more repeat briefly what those achievements were, because they were so great and splendid, and because no other sailor has ever so greatly enlarged the borders of the earth. He discovered the Society Islands; he proved New Zealand to be two islands and he surveyed its coasts; he followed the unknown coast of New Holland for two thousand miles and proved that it was separated from New Guinea; he traversed the Antarctic Ocean on three successive voyages, sailing completely round the globe in its high latitudes, and proving that the dream of the great southern continent had no foundation, unless it was close around the Pole and so beyond the reach of ships; he discovered and explored a great part of the coast of New Caledonia, the largest island in the South Pacific next to New Zealand; he found the desolate island of Georgia, and Sandwich land, the southernmost land yet known; he discovered the fair and fertile archipelago called the Sandwich Islands; he explored three thousand five hundred miles of the North American coast, and he traversed the icy seas of the North Pacific, as he had done in the south, in search of the passage which he failed to discover. All this, without counting the small islands which he found scattered about the Pacific.

Again, he not only proved the existence of these islands, but he was in advance of his age in the observations and the minute examination which he made into the religion, manners, customs, arts, and language of the natives wherever he went. It was he who directed these inquiries, and he was himself the principal observer. When astronomical observations had to be made it was he who acted as principal astronomer. He was as much awake to the importance of botany, especially of medicinal plants, as he was to the laying down of a correct chart. It is certain that there was not in the whole of the king's navy any officer who could compare with Cook in breadth and depth of knowledge, in forethought, in the power of conceiving great designs, and in courage and pertinacity in carrying them through. Let us always think of the captain growing only more cheerful as his ship forced her way southwards, though his men lay half-starved and half-poisoned on the deck.

His voyages would have been impossible, his discoveries could not have been made, but for that invaluable discovery of his whereby scurvy was kept off and the men enabled to remain at sea long months without a change. I have called attention to the brief mention he makes of privation and hardships; he barely notes the accident by which half his company were poisoned by fish, he says nothing about the men's discomforts when their biscuit was rotten. These things, you see, are not scurvy. One may go hungry for a while, but recover when food is found and is none the worse; one gets sick of salt junk, but if scurvy is averted, mere disgust is not worth observation. To drive off scurvy, to keep it off, was the greatest boon that any man could confer upon sailors. Cook has the honour and glory of finding out the way to avert this scourge. Those who have read of this horrible disease, the tortures it entailed, the terror it was on all long voyages, will understand how great should be the gratitude of the country to this man. Since the disease fell chiefly upon the men before the mast, it was fitting that one who had also in his youth run up the rigging to the music of the boatswain's pipe should discover that way and confer that boon.

The gratitude of Cook's country was shown in several ways, all rather curious. Had he been a member of a noble family his son would certainly have been raised to the peerage. As he was not, the king granted his family a coat of arms. I think that this must have been the last occasion when a coat of arms was granted as a recognition of service. In these days, if a man wants a coat of arms, he gets some one who understands heraldry to draw him one or to find him one, or perhaps he ignorantly tries to make one for himself. A coat of arms; such a grant seems now to mean nothing. We think we can confer gentility upon ourselves, as, indeed, for all practical purposes we can; but not of the ancient kind. The old notion that gentility can be conferred by the sovereign as the fountain of honour is clean forgotten. But it was not then forgotten. No man could make himself *armiger*. Cook's family, therefore, were rewarded with a shield: they were advanced to the first step of nobility. The shield is thus described.

Azure, between the two polar stars Or, a sphere on the plane of the meridian, shewing the Pacific Ocean, his track thereon marked by red lines. And for crest, on a wreath of the colours, is an arm bowed, in the uniform of a Captain of the Royal Navy. In the hand is the Union Jack on a staff proper. The arm is encircled by a wreath of palm and laurel.

A very noble shield indeed!

A pension of two hundred pounds a year was bestowed upon the widow, and the Government further bestowed upon her half the profits arising from the publication of her husband's Journal of the Third Voyage. She also received a share in the profits of the Journal of the Second Voyage, but in both cases the interest alone was to be hers for life, the children to receive the principal after her death. At their death the principal was paid to her. Mrs. Cook was thus left fully provided for. It only remains to tell the story of the fate which fell upon Cook's children as well as upon himself. There were six children in all. Three died in infancy or in tender years. Three grew up to manhood. Of these the eldest, James, was in the navy. The second, Nathaniel, also went into the navy. The third and youngest, Hugh, was sent to Cambridge, where he entered at Christ's College in the year 1793.

I have before me a copy of Captain Cook's will. The amount for which it was proved is not stated. He bequeaths an annuity of £10 to his father, certain bequests of £10 each to nephews and nieces, and the rest, including his messuages at Mile End Town, to his wife. He was thus, before starting on his last voyage, possessed of substantial means.

The news of her husband's death reached the unhappy widow in the first week of October 1780. In the same week her second son Nathaniel went down on board the *Thunderer* in a hurricane off Jamaica. The news reached her before the end of the year. Then followed a period of thirteen years, during which she saw her eldest son from time to time, a gallant and active officer, always on service, and educated the youngest boy, Hugh. In July 1793 this son, as I have said, was entered as a pensioner at Christ's, and went into residence in October. Two months later he was attacked by scarlet fever, and died on December 21st in his eighteenth year. A portrait of this unfortunate youth in the possession of Canon Bennett shows a face of very remarkable beauty and delicacy, with none of the severity which belonged to that of his father.

Only five weeks later another blow fell upon the hapless woman, already bereaved of husband and five out of her six children. Her eldest son, who had been in the autumn of 1793 promoted to the rank of commander, was, while with his ship at Poole, in Dorsetshire, appointed to the command of the *Spitfire* sloop of war. On January 24th, 1794, he received from Captain Yeo, commanding officer of the station, his letters and orders to take command without delay. He started immediately in an open boat, manned by sailors returning from leave, to sail from Poole to Portsmouth. It was in the afternoon. His boat was rather crowded: there was a strong ebb tide and a fresh wind; it was growing dark. This was the last seen of James Cook, the younger.

For he never reached his ship. What happened will never now be known. His body, with a wound on the head and stripped of all his money and valuables, was found on the beach at the back of the Isle of Wight; the boat was also found broken up; but no trace of any of the crew was discovered. Perhaps they were drowned. Perhaps they murdered the captain, made for the island, laid his body on the beach, broke up the boat, and dispersed.

The body was brought over to Portsmouth and taken to Cambridge, where it was laid in the same grave with the remains of his brother Hugh.

Overwhelmed by this final blow, the unhappy woman was prostrated with an illness of mind and body which kept her to her house for two years. When she recovered she asked her cousin, Admiral Isaac Smith, who was unmarried, to live with her. They took a house together at Clapham, where she continued to live until her death in 1835, being then ninety-three years of age. By her own request she was buried with her two sons in the centre aisle of St. Andrew's Church, Cambridge.

She kept her faculties to the end. My informant describes her as a handsome and venerable lady, her white hair rolled back in ancient fashion, always dressed in black satin, with an oval face, an aquiline nose, and a good mouth. She wore a ring with her husband's hair in it; and she entertained the highest respect for his memory, measuring everything by his standard of honour and morality. Her keenest expression of disapprobation was that Mr. Cook, to her he was always Mr. Cook, not Captain, "would never have done so."

Like many widows of sailors, she could never sleep in high wind for thinking of the men at sea, and she kept four days in the year of solemn fasting, during which she came not out of her own room: they were the days of her bereavements; the days when she lost her husband and her three boys. She passed those days in prayer and meditation with her husband's Bible; and for her husband's sake she befriended their nephews and grand-nephews and nieces and grand-nieces of his whom she never saw; they were not suffered to want.

With her pension and her share of the profits of the books and with other things, such as the inheritance of her sailor son's fortune, sworn under £5000, Mrs. Cook became a wealthy woman. Her house was good, and filled with old furniture of the style called Louis Quinze; it was also crowded and crammed in every room with relics, curiosities, drawings, maps, and collections brought home from the voyages. It would seem that the Government gave back the drawings and charts after they had been published. On Thursdays she always entertained her friends to dinner, which was served at three o'clock. After the death of her cousin the admiral she was taken care of by a faithful old servant whom she remembered in her will, and by younger members of her own family.

The greater part of the relics preserved were sent to the Colonial Government Museum, Sydney, after the Colonial Exhibition. But the log of the First Voyage and the gold medal conferred on the captain by the Royal Society are in the British Museum.

The following genealogy shows the numbers and the end of Cook's family. All, as has been seen, were cut off in youth or infancy, and no descendant now survives of England's greatest navigator.

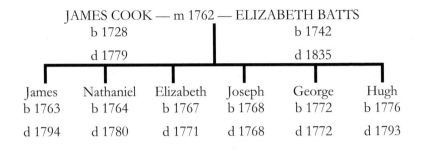

JAMES COOK — m 1762 — ELIZABETH BATTS
b 1728   b 1742
d 1779   d 1835

James	Nathaniel	Elizabeth	Joseph	George	Hugh
b 1763	b 1764	b 1767	b 1768	b 1772	b 1776
d 1794	d 1780	d 1771	d 1768	d 1772	d 1793

For these personal recollections of Mrs. Cook, and also for various documents connected with her husband's domestic life, I am indebted to Canon Bennett, of Maddington Vicarage, Devizes. As he is probably the only survivor of her personal friends, this information could not have been procured from any one else; without it the history of Cook's private life would have been indeed shadowy.

THE END